sugar-free
snacks&treats

sugar-free
snacks&treats

Deliciously tempting bites that are free from refined sugars

RYLAND PETERS & SMALL
LONDON • NEW YORK

Designer Luana Gobbo
Editor Kate Eddison
Production David Hearn
Art Director Leslie Harrington
Editorial Director Julia Charles
Publisher Cindy Richards

Indexer Hilary Bird

First published in 2015
by Ryland Peters & Small,
20–21 Jockey's Fields,
London WC1R 4BW
and
341 E 116th St
New York NY 10029
www.rylandpeters.com

10 9 8 7 6 5 4 3 2 1

Printed in China

ISBN: 978-1-84975-603-7

A CIP record for this book is available from the
British Library.

US Library of Congress CIP data has been applied for.

Note
• Both British (Metric) and American (Imperial plus
  US cups) are included in these recipes for your
  convenience, however it is important to work with
  one set of measurements and not alternate
  between the two within a recipe.
• All spoon measurements are level unless otherwise
  specified.
• All eggs are medium (UK) or large (US), unless
  specified as large, in which case US extra-large
  should be used. Uncooked or partially cooked eggs
  should not be served to the very old, frail, young
  children, pregnant women or those with
  compromised immune systems.
• When a recipe calls for the grated zest of citrus
  fruit, buy unwaxed fruit and wash well before
  using. If you can only find treated fruit, scrub well
  in warm soapy water before using.
• Ovens should be preheated to the specified
  temperatures. We recommend using an oven
  thermometer. If using a fan-assisted oven, adjust
  temperatures according to the manufacturer's
  instructions.
• Most dark/bittersweet chocolate that contains
  70% cocoa solids is dairy-free, but you will need
  to check what it's sweetened with. Nowadays
  there are plenty of brands that use xylitol, stevia,
  and various kinds of fruit sugars in their chocolates.

contents

introduction

The health hazards of sugar are well known. High consumption of sugar has been shown to correlate with the big killers: heart disease, diabetes and cancer. While these are not necessarily factors people think about every day, refined white sugar throws our bodies off course. The body likes to have even blood sugar, control of its moods and steady energy levels, but sugar interrupts this preferred happy state. Ingesting refined sugars places such a heavy burden on the body, it has to work extra hard to stay happy.

Having said that, we all love a sweet treat. Lots of people try to cut out sugar in their diets, but it is the times when we want a quick energy boost or a tasty pick-me-up that it is difficult to avoid the processed white grains. Store-bought confections, cookies, crackers and nibbles tend to be packed with refined sugars, and savoury snacks are just as guilty. Luckily, there are amazing alternatives available to us nowadays that are much gentler on our bodies, so we can still eat luxurious and tasty treats without the negative effects on our health. Food should be enjoyed without guilt, and this book allows you to do just that!

replacing sugar

There are plenty of healthier alternatives to sugar out there. In order to cover your bases, it's a good idea to find both a liquid sweetener and a granulated sweetener that you like, because they behave differently when cooked. Where a conventional recipe calls for white sugar, for example, using agave syrup in its place will affect the moisture and texture of the finished product.

Despite its unusual name, xylitol does not belong to the class of 'artificial sweeteners' that have received bad press in recent years for their possible side-effects. It is a sweetener that the body recognizes as natural because it is present in all plant cells and is derived from tree bark. It can be used in the same way as sugar and has no impact on blood sugar levels. It also doesn't feed mouth bacteria, which means it is a better option than sugar for dental health.

Coconut palm sugar has a lower GI than sugar cane and is full of vitamins and minerals that will have a beneficial impact on your health, while satisfying your cravings. Agave, maple, date and rice syrups are all low-GI liquid sugar alternatives that will not cause blood sugar levels to sky rocket.

Alternative sweeteners have all been criticized at some point for not being as healthy as they claim, but it's important to remember that these are meant to be used in moderation and regarded as a 'treat' food. Use your head, do your research and choose minimally processed ingredients wherever possible. At the end of the day, sugar in any form should not be the mainstay of our diet, but when you do feel like a treat, you can have something that will be far better for your health than the typical offerings, yet just as tasty.

Dark/bittersweet chocolate

Most people assume they can't have chocolate when trying to cut down on sugar. You'll find that most dark/bittersweet chocolate that contains 70% cocoa solids is dairy-free, but you will need to check what it's sweetened with. Nowadays there are plenty of brands that use xylitol, stevia, and various kinds of fruit sugars in their chocolates. Chocolate chips are good for baking purposes, and they melt really easily too.

Substituting ingredients

In almost all of the recipes in this book, you can use liquid sweeteners interchangeably – maple syrup is delicious, but you can use agave syrup, brown rice syrup or honey according to your preferences and your needs. When baking, though, you can't substitute a liquid sweetener for a granulated sweetener or vice versa.

When it comes to granulated sweeteners, there's a little wiggle room in substituting one for the other, but it's worth remembering that stevia (a natural and calorie-free sweetener derived from a plant) is a lot sweeter than fruit sugar (such as Fruisana), coconut sugar and xylitol, which are in turn sweeter than white sugar, so you're safer sticking to xylitol or fruit sugar when the recipe calls for it. The other thing about stevia is that it can taste a little weird when cooked. For this reason it is best reserved for cold drinks and foods that have to be refrigerated or frozen to set. You can feel free to use fruit sugar, xylitol, palm sugar and coconut sugar interchangeably though. The latter two have a caramel-like taste that you can use to alter flavour where you like.

Avoiding wheat or dairy

There are so many approaches to 'healthy' snacks and everyone has different priorities that suit their lifestyle. Many of the recipes in this book are also free from refined white flour, gluten and dairy. Once you get the hang of different ingredients, you can substitute effectively to make the recipes suit your needs.

Perhaps the hardest ingredient to substitute effectively is flour. This is because flour can be made from almost any grain, bean or nut, all of which cook at varying rates. Where a recipe calls for chickpea flour and you sub it for brown rice flour, it may make all the difference between a gorgeous cake and a chalky mess. You also run the risk of the flour cooking way faster or slower than the other ingredients involved, which doesn't make for good results taste-wise. Look for a good gluten-free plain/all-purpose flour to use where grain flours are called for. If you are keen to see how a particular flour you love would work in a recipe, though, you can play around with things – in fact that's half the fun! You just have to be open to trying and tweaking a couple of times before you reach your desired outcome.

For savoury and non-baking recipes, it's particularly easy – and usually successful! – to ring the changes and experiment with the nuts, seeds, fruits and vegetables. Be brave and work with what you have to hand!

savoury snacks

Homemade snacks are always 150% healthier than anything you can buy in the supermarkets or your local store, so why snack on oily chips, processed and additive-rich pretzels, sticks, and so on, when you can make your own tasty bites for the whole family to enjoy?

cracker snacks with black sesame seeds

MAKES 16–18

260 g/2 cups flour of your choice, or a combination of 2–3 different kinds, if you like, chilled

¼ teaspoon sea salt

4 teaspoons baking powder

140 g/1 cup non-hydrogenated margarine, chilled

1 tablespoon brown rice syrup

50 ml/¼ cup ice-cold plain soy milk or water, or as needed

For the topping

black sesame seeds (or other seeds or dried herbs, such as sesame, caraway, cumin, dried oregano, dried basil, etc.)

coarse sea salt

Put the flour, salt and baking powder in a food processor and pulse to mix. Add the margarine and pulse 6–8 times until the mixture resembles coarse breadcrumbs. Add the syrup and pulse again a couple of times. Gradually add the ice-cold milk or water one tablespoon at a time, pulsing until the mixture just begins to clump together. If you pinch some of the crumbly dough and it holds together, it's ready. If the dough doesn't hold together, add a little more liquid and pulse again. Be careful not to add too much, or it will make the crackers tough.

Place the dough on a lightly floured work surface. Knead it just enough to form a ball but do not over-knead it. Shape it into a disc, wrap it in clingfilm/plastic wrap and refrigerate it for at least 1 hour, and up to 2 days. If you're in a hurry you can chill the dough in the freezer for 15 minutes. Allow the dough to rest at room temperature for 5–10 minutes before rolling it out.

Preheat the oven to 180°C (350°F) Gas 4.

Place the dough on a sheet of lightly floured parchment paper, dust with a little flour and roll it out with a rolling pin until 1 mm/¹⁄₃₂ inch thick. Use a pastry wheel to cut it into short or long sticks, or you could stamp out shapes with a cookie cutter. Slide the crackers and paper onto a baking sheet. Separate each cracker so they don't stick together during baking.

For the topping, lightly brush each cracker with water and sprinkle the black sesame seeds over the top. Salt lightly.

Bake in the preheated oven for 10 minutes, or until the dough puffs up a little and turns golden. Allow to cool completely on the baking sheet. Store in an airtight container for up to 2 weeks.

Buckwheat is a really healthy seed that is often overlooked, but it's a big shame not to eat it from time to time! Try these crackers as a snack topped with chutney or roasted vegetables.

buckwheat crackers

MAKES 15

95 g/½ cup buckwheat

85 g/⅔ cup sunflower seeds

100 g/1 cup grated vegetables or leftover pulp

¾ teaspoon sea salt

1 medium red (bell) pepper, seeded

60 g/½ cup diced onion

½ teaspoon dried oregano

¼ teaspoon dried thyme

¼ teaspoon dried basil

2 tablespoons ground flaxseed

3 tablespoons olive oil

110 ml/½ cup vegetable juice or water

Preheat the oven to 80°C (175°F) Gas ⅛.

In a high-speed blender, mix all the ingredients into a thick paste. Cut a piece of parchment paper to the size of your oven shelf/rack or baking pan and place it on a smooth surface. Spoon the paste so that it's about 3 mm/⅛ inch thick onto the parchment paper in a large rectangle. Put the oven shelf/rack or baking pan on the edge of your kitchen counter and quickly pull the parchment paper to slide it on. Place the oven shelf/rack or baking pan in the upper part of the oven; turn the heat up to 100°C (210°F) Gas ¼, but prop the door open with a folded tea/dish towel, to ensure proper dehydration of the buckwheat. Dehydrate for 2–3 hours.

Peel off the parchment paper and use a pizza cutter to cut the crackers into the desired shape; dehydrate the crackers directly on the oven shelf/rack for another 30 minutes if you want them really crispy. They are delicious a bit on the soft side, but dry crackers last longer without spoiling. Spoon on some chutney or roasted veggies to serve.

A lot of us are intimidated by bread-baking's reputation for being complicated and time-consuming but this recipe is easier than you might think. Make the breadsticks thick so that they're crunchy on the outside but soft on the inside.

rosemary breadsticks

MAKES 12–14

180 ml/¾ cup lukewarm water

1 teaspoon fast-action dried yeast

½ teaspoon agave syrup or honey

300 g/3 cups gluten-free plain/all-purpose flour of choice, plus extra for dusting

3 teaspoons xanthan gum

1½ teaspoons sea salt

2 tablespoons extra virgin olive oil

leaves from a few sprigs of fresh rosemary (dried is fine too, if you don't have fresh), coarsely chopped

2 baking sheets lined with foil

Put the warm water and yeast in a very large bowl and mix well until the yeast has dissolved. Stir in the agave syrup or honey – this small amount of sweetness helps feed the yeast, which is crucial in making the dough rise. Allow it to rest for 5 minutes.

Separately, sift together the flour, xanthan gum and salt, making sure the xanthan gum is well distributed.

Add the olive oil to the yeast mixture, then sift the dry ingredients into it, stirring well to avoid any lumps. Add the rosemary and make sure it is well incorporated. You should see a big ball of dough starting to form.

Dust a clean surface with flour and place the dough ball on it. Knead the dough for 10 minutes and flour your surface generously as you go along. You want to gently stretch the dough with your hands and fold it over itself, and repeat this action in different directions.

Roll the dough with a rolling pin into a rough circle about 30 cm/ 12 inches wide. Make sure the surface is nice and flat. Cover the dough tightly with clingfilm/plastic wrap, followed by a damp kitchen towel, and let it sit for about 90 minutes.

About 15 minutes before you are ready to bake the sticks, preheat the oven to 200°C (400°F) Gas 6.

Uncover the dough; it should have risen to double its height. Cut it in half, then cut each half into 4 long slices so you have 8 strips. The strips on the outer ends of the circle should be a perfect length for breadsticks, but you should cut the longer ones in half again. Roll each strip out with your hands to lengthen and thin it to your preferred size. Gently twist the sticks and place them on the prepared baking sheets.

Place one baking sheet on the top rack and the other on the middle rack of the preheated oven and bake for 15 minutes. Swap the sheets around and bake for another 10 minutes. Allow to cool slightly before eating. Store in an airtight container for up to 2 days.

Tortilla chips and salsa are the snack you just can't stop eating once you start. And with this recipe, there's no reason why you should stop – it's one of the most delicious combos ever invented, and you can rest assured you're eating only good stuff. There aren't several teaspoons of hidden sugar in this salsa, which is plenty sweet enough from the addition of a nectarine.

baked tortilla chips with nectarine-tomato salsa

Stack the tortillas on a board and cut through them into eighths to make wedges. Scatter the wedges over the prepared baking sheets and sprinkle with the salt. Bake in the preheated oven, one baking sheet at a time, for 13 minutes – don't bake both at the same time because the bottom sheet of tortillas will inevitably undercook. Thirteen minutes is really the golden number – any longer and the tortillas will become impossible to chew; any less and they won't get crunchy.

For the nectarine-tomato salsa, dice the nectarine, cherry tomatoes, red onion and jalapeño, if using, and combine with the remaining ingredients. Now put half of the mixture in a food processor, blitz until smooth, then add it to the unblended mixture. This half-blending trick makes the perfect salsa – mostly smooth and easy to scoop onto a tortilla chip, but with enough chunks for you to be able to taste all the components. Yum!

SERVES 6–8

10–12 all-corn tortillas

1 teaspoon sea salt

For the nectarine-tomato salsa

1 nectarine

450 g/1 lb. cherry tomatoes

½ red onion

½ fresh jalapeño pepper (optional)

3 tablespoons freshly chopped coriander/cilantro

1 teaspoon chilli/chili powder

1 lime

2 tablespoons apple cider vinegar

2 baking sheets lined with foil

The perfect combination of sweet, salty and spicy. Popcorn and a fizzy drink, made the healthy way, with home-popped corn without any added fat, and no nasties from the sugary sodas.

cinema snacks, revisited

SERVES 1

For the masala popcorn

1 tablespoon corn kernels

½ teaspoon sea salt

1 tablespoon chaat masala (to make your own, mix a pinch each of garam masala, ground cumin, ground fennel seeds, ground ginger, ground black pepper and paprika)

For the fizzy lemonade

ice, to serve

500 ml/2 cups naturally sparkling water

freshly squeezed juice of ½ lemon

1 teaspoon xylitol or stevia

For the masala popcorn, put the corn kernels in a non-stick saucepan over medium heat and place the lid on top. As soon as you hear the corn start to pop, turn the heat down to low. Remove when all corn has popped – about 45–60 seconds. Toss the freshly popped corn with the salt and chaat masala and place in a big bowl. You have full permission to eat the entire serving yourself!

For the fizzy lemonade, put some ice in a large glass and pour in the sparkling water and lemon juice. Add the sweetener and stir well.

Variations

Basil and oregano: add 1 teaspoon olive oil to the corn kernels in the pan. Pop as above, then remove from the heat and toss in 1 tablespoon each of dried basil and dried oregano.

Cheesy truffle: add 1 teaspoon truffle-infused olive oil to the corn kernels in the pan. Pop as above, then remove from the heat and toss in 3 teaspoons nutritional yeast, which will give the popcorn a slightly cheesy flavour.

Sweet treat: add 1 teaspoon coconut oil mixed with 1 teaspoon vanilla extract to the corn kernels in the pan. Pop as above, then remove from the heat and toss in a generous pinch of ground cinnamon.

This version of New York-style sweet glazed nuts is pretty authentic.
The recipe uses ground almonds/almond meal in place of white sugar to give
them that slightly gritty texture that the classic ones have too. Fill small paper
cones with these irresistible nuts and you'll soon be transported to the
bustling streets of New York City.

NYC-style glazed nuts

SERVES 6

2 tablespoons coconut oil

2 tablespoons agave syrup
(agave is slightly stickier
than other liquid
sweeteners)

1 teaspoon grated nutmeg

350 g/about 2½ cups mixed
nuts, such as almonds,
peanuts, cashews,
hazelnuts, soy nuts

2 tablespoons xylitol or
stevia, or other granulated
sweetener

½ teaspoon arrowroot or
cornflour/cornstarch

50 g/½ cup ground almonds/
almond meal

baking sheet lined with foil

Preheat the oven to 200°C (400°F) Gas 6.

Put the coconut oil in a medium saucepan and heat until melted.
Remove from the heat and allow it to cool for a few minutes, then stir in
the agave syrup and grated nutmeg.

Add the nuts to the saucepan and toss to coat well in the liquid. Using
a slotted spoon, transfer the nuts to a bowl. Reserve the remaining liquid
in the pan for later.

Put the sweetener and arrowroot or cornflour/cornstarch in a high-speed
blender and blitz until finely ground. Combine this with the ground
almonds/almond meal, then tip into the bowl of nuts. Mix well to coat,
then transfer the nuts to the prepared baking sheet. Pour the reserved
liquid over the nuts and toss them.

Roast the nuts in the preheated oven for 30 minutes, then allow to cool
for 5 minutes before serving. Store in an airtight container for up to 5 days.

SERVES 8

3–4 tablespoons
  peanut/groundnut oil
  (or almond oil, coconut oil
  or grapeseed oil)

70 g/½ cup yellow split peas

35 g/¼ cup cashews

35 g/¼ cup peanuts

35 g/¼ cup pumpkin seeds

110 g/2 cups plain cornflakes
  (with no added sugar)

3 tablespoons unsweetened
  flaked coconut

3–4 slices dried mango, finely
  chopped

2 tablespoons raisins

½ teaspoon ground cumin

¼ teaspoon paprika

1 teaspoon ground turmeric

½ teaspoon sea salt

½ teaspoon onion powder

2 teaspoons Worcestershire
  sauce

freshly squeezed juice of
  1 lime

1 fresh green chilli/chile,
  deseeded and sliced

1 tablespoon water (optional)

Who doesn't love a good salty bar snack? Here is a version you don't have to feel guilty about, and it won't leave you feeling sluggish afterwards.

The list of ingredients is long, but don't be put off – the whole thing takes about 10 minutes to prepare, and if you don't have some of the components, feel free to omit them.

bombay mix

Heat the oil in a saucepan over medium heat. Fry the split peas, cashews, peanuts and pumpkin seeds for a few minutes until the split peas have softened and are cooked through. Add the corn flakes and toss until crispy.

Add all the remaining ingredients. If the mixture gets dry, feel free to drizzle in the tablespoon of water. Stir to combine, remove from the heat and discard any remaining moisture or oil.

Allow to cool, then refrigerate in an airtight container until you're ready to serve it. It will keep for up to 1 week. If it softens after a few days, toast it slightly in the oven.

These savoury pancakes made from gram (chickpea) flour, olive oil and water hail from the Côte d'Azur in the south of France. They are naturally wheat and gluten free, and can be topped with just about anything you like, but the combination of chopped parsley, olives and red onion works wonderfully well.

socca

SERVES 6

For the socca

150 g/generous 1 cup gram (chickpea) flour

½ teaspoon salt

½ teaspoon ground turmeric

3 tablespoons extra virgin olive oil

sunflower oil, for frying

For the topping

handful of pitted black and green olives, chopped into small chunks

2 tablespoons freshly chopped parsley

1 red onion, very finely chopped

1 lemon

sea salt and freshly ground black pepper

extra virgin olive oil

To make the socca, sift the gram flour into a bowl and add the salt and turmeric. Slowly add 380 ml/1⅔ cups water, whisking quickly all the time until all the water has been added, breaking up any lumps of flour as you go. Add the olive oil and stir.

Heat a little sunflower oil in a 20-cm/8-in. non-stick frying pan/skillet until hot. Pour a ladleful of the batter into the pan, swirling it so that the mixture spreads to the edges. Reduce the heat to low–medium and cook gently. It will take a good 6–8 minutes on the first side. Resist the temptation to stick your spatula underneath it until the edges have completely dried out and the middle has tiny little bubbles. At this point, take the pan and shake from side to side. The pancake should move, but if it is sticking, you can help it along gently with a spatula. However, if it is not budging at all, leave it for another minute and then try again. Flip the pancake and cook for a further 1–2 minutes. The second side does not need to be cooked for as long, as it is nice if it is still a little soft.

Repeat until all the batter has been used up, wrapping the pancakes in parchment paper and keeping them warm in a low oven.

For the topping, liberally scatter the chopped olives, parsley and onion over the pancakes. Season with a good pinch of salt and pepper, a drizzle of extra virgin olive oil and a squeeze of lemon juice.

Cut the pancakes into wedges, as they do in the south of France, or you can roll them up into big cigars. A little bit of hummus plopped on top works really well too, if you are so inclined.

Onion rings evoke a whimsical, 1950s American playfulness and the importance of the vibe around our food cannot be ignored. Enjoy dipped in Healthified Ketchup (below).

jalapeño onion rings

MAKES ABOUT 3 DOZEN

3 tablespoons ground flaxseeds/linseeds

170 g/1 cup cornmeal

150 g/1 cup gluten-free crackers, processed into crumbs

1 large fresh jalapeño pepper, thinly sliced and deseeded if you don't like things too spicy

½ teaspoon sea salt

freshly ground black pepper

2 large onions, cut into 2-cm/1-in. thick slices

2 baking sheets lined with foil

Preheat the oven to 220°C (425°F) Gas 7.

Mix the flaxseeds/linseeds and 175 ml/⅔ cup water. Set aside. Separately, mix the cornmeal, cracker crumbs, jalapeño, salt, and pepper to taste in a wide bowl. Separate the onion slices into rings.

Dip the onion slices into the flaxseed/linseed mixture, then into the crumb mixture. For each onion ring, do this twice so that they are double-coated.

Arrange the rings on the prepared baking sheets and bake in the preheated oven for 8–12 minutes until they are slightly browned on the outside and cooked all the way through. Serve with Healthified Ketchup (below).

Super simple to make your own, keep a batch of this in your refrigerator to eat with grilled courgettes/zucchini, corn, veggie burgers and, of course, Jalapeño Onion Rings (above).

healthified ketchup

MAKES ABOUT 1 CUPFUL

250 ml/1 cup plain tomato passata/strained tomatoes

1 teaspoon celery salt or Herbamare

½ teaspoon garlic powder

1 teaspoon onion powder

1 tablespoon xylitol

1 tablespoon apple cider vinegar

4 teaspoons cornflour/cornstarch

Put the passata, celery salt, garlic powder, onion powder, xylitol and vinegar in a saucepan over medium heat. Heat gently for about 15 minutes without letting it boil. Separately, mix the cornflour/cornstarch with 2 tablespoons water in a small bowl or cup until combined.

Taste the tomato mixture in the pan and add more salt or xylitol to taste. Remove from the stove and stir in the cornflour/cornstarch mixture. As you stir, it will start to thicken until you get that authentic ketchup texture. Store in an airtight container in the refrigerator for up to 1 week.

SERVES 3–4

80 ml/⅓ cup almond milk

35 g/¼ cup quinoa flour

35 g/¼ cup ground
flaxseeds/linseeds

1 teaspoon garlic powder

½ teaspoon onion powder

½ teaspoon freshly ground
black pepper

½ teaspoon sea salt

2 large courgettes/zucchini,
cut into 5-mm/¼-in. slices

*baking sheet lined with
parchment paper*

If you have a weakness for the fried courgette/zucchini side dish that most Italian restaurants offer, try this baked version instead. Once you have one of these, you can't stop eating them. The health benefits of this version have been boosted by the addition of Omega-3s in the form of ground flaxseeds/linseeds. Eat these as a snack or serve them alongside your healthy dinner.

If you wanted a spicier version, you could substitute the onion powder and black pepper for some cayenne pepper.

courgette UN-fries

Preheat the oven to 220°C (425°F) Gas 7.

Put the almond milk in a bowl and set aside. Put all the remaining ingredients (except the courgettes/zucchini) in a separate, wide bowl and mix well.

Place each slice of courgette/zucchini into the almond milk, one at a time, then dip into the dry mixture. Once fully coated, place on the prepared baking sheet.

Bake the UN-fries in the preheated oven for 15 minutes. Remove from the oven, flip the slices over, and bake for another 15 minutes. Keep a close eye on them, as they burn easily. They can be served warm from the oven or at room temperature.

SERVES 3–4

1 large head cauliflower,
cut into florets about
1 cm/½ in. thick

2 tablespoons black
treacle/molasses or
maple syrup

4–5 tablespoons tomato
passata/strained tomatoes
(or 1 tablespoon tomato
purée/paste mixed with
4 tablespoons water if you
don't have passata on hand)

1 teaspoon cayenne pepper

2 teaspoons paprika

1 teaspoon ground cumin

½ teaspoon dried thyme

½ teaspoon garlic powder

1 teaspoon sea salt

freshly ground black pepper

*baking sheet lined with
parchment paper*

A few years ago, 'cauliflower popcorn' started popping up in raw food circles. The idea was that you could dehydrate tiny pieces of cauliflower until crunchy, like popcorn. This version has a little more zing. You do have to make this ahead of time, as it takes about 6 hours in the oven or dehydrator.

creole cauliflower

Preheat the oven to 115°C (225°F) Gas ¼, with the fan on if possible.

Wash the cauliflower florets thoroughly, then place in a large bowl. Put all the remaining ingredients in a separate, wide bowl and mix well. Pour the mixture over the cauliflower in the bowl and toss until well coated.

Scatter the cauliflower on a baking sheet and bake in the preheated oven for about 6 hours, until thoroughly dried and crisp.

dips and
small bites

You eat with your eyes with this dip! Beetroot is as nutritious as it is colourful. Sumac is a great North African and Middle Eastern spice, also used in the spice blend za'atar. Seeds make nutty and delicious crackers and you can make a cracker purely from seeds, but the addition of a bit of amaranth flour gives the crackers a little more substance while still retaining a crispy texture.

beetroot herb dip with seeded amaranth crackers

SERVES 4

For the beetroot herb dip

2 garlic bulbs, unpeeled

4 beetroot/beets, tops and bottoms trimmed

3 tablespoons flaxseed oil

1½ teaspoons ground sumac

1 teaspoon cumin seeds

freshly squeezed juice of 1 lemon

1 teaspoon sea salt

freshly ground black pepper

handful of fresh coriander/ cilantro, to garnish

For the amaranth crackers

45 g/⅓ cup amaranth flour

40 g/⅓ cup milled flaxseeds/ linseeds

40 g/¼ cup sunflower seeds

1 teaspoon sea salt

¼ teaspoon onion powder or ½ small chopped onion

20 g/⅛ cup pumpkin seeds

2 tablespoons milled hemp seeds

1 tablespoon melted coconut oil, plus extra for greasing

2 baking sheets lined with foil

For the dip, preheat the oven to 180°C (350°F) Gas 4.

Wrap the garlic in foil and put on one of the prepared baking sheets. Wrap the beetroot/beets in a separate sheet of foil and put on the same baking sheet. Roast the beetroot/beets and garlic for 30 minutes, then remove the garlic and set aside. Roast the beetroot/beets for a further 30 minutes or until tender, then allow to cool.

Peel the garlic and the beetroot/beets (this is the messy part so feel free to wear gloves!) and blend them in a food processor with the flaxseed oil, sumac, cumin seeds, lemon juice, salt and pepper. Add more flaxseed oil as required to reach the desired consistency.

For the crackers, preheat the oven to 150°C (300°F) Gas 2. Grease the second prepared baking sheet with a thin layer of coconut oil.

Pulse all of the dry ingredients in a food processor – you can leave the seeds in a roughly chopped state, if you prefer more texture. Then add the coconut oil and 4 tablespoons water, and blend again until all the ingredients come together into a dough. Roll the dough thinly onto the prepared baking sheet and bake for 45–50 minutes. Set aside to cool, then break into pieces. Store in an airtight container until ready to serve.

Transfer the dip to a serving bowl, garnish with fresh coriander/cilantro and serve with the crackers.

Edamame (soy) beans are full of calcium and are a rare plant source of Omega-3 fatty acids. This dip is a fun way to consume them. Eat it with cut veggies or in a sandwich with avocado, cucumber, carrots and ginger.

edamame and miso dip

MAKES 1 CUPFUL

- 200 g/1½ cups shelled edamame beans (fresh, or frozen and thawed)
- 3 tablespoons sweet white miso paste
- 1 tablespoon extra virgin olive oil
- 1 tablespoon tamari soy sauce
- 1 teaspoon wasabi paste

Put nearly all the edamame beans (reserving some for decoration) and 1 tablespoon water in a food processor and blitz until smooth. Add the remaining ingredients and mix well so that everything is well incorporated.

Decorate with the reserved edamame beans. Store in an airtight container in the refrigerator for up to 5 days.

If you're a hummus purist, this version may not satisfy you in the same way, but using courgettes/zucchini instead of chickpeas can be a really nice way to change things slightly. Because it's also completely bean free, it makes a great alternative for those who have trouble digesting them. Professional hummus makers add ice cubes to their recipes to add to the texture of fresh hummus – try it and see what you think.

courgette hummus

MAKES 1 CUPFUL

- 2 courgettes/zucchini
- 80 ml/⅓ cup tahini paste
- 2–3 ice cubes
- 1 garlic clove
- freshly squeezed juice of ½ lemon, plus extra to preserve
- a pinch of sea salt
- 1 teaspoon smoked paprika
- 1 tablespoon extra virgin olive oil

food processor that can crush ice cubes

If you want the colour of your dip to resemble traditional hummus, peel the courgettes/zucchini. If not, keep the skins on for added vitamins and minerals.

Roughly chop the courgettes/zucchini and put in a food processor with the tahini, ice cubes, garlic clove, lemon juice, salt and half the paprika. Pulse until completely smooth.

Garnish with the rest of the paprika and the olive oil. Squeeze lemon juice over the top to prevent it from browning and store in an airtight container in the refrigerator for up to 5 days.

sweet potato hummus

ALL RECIPES SERVE 8

1 large sweet potato, baked

400-g/14-oz. can chickpeas

2 garlic cloves, peeled

100 ml/6 tablespoons tahini

½ teaspoon each cumin and coriander seeds, gently toasted in a dry pan

grated zest and juice of ½ lemon

sea salt

extra virgin olive oil

1 tablespoon freshly chopped parsley

Scoop the flesh out of the potato. Put the flesh, chickpeas (reserving a few to garnish), garlic and tahini in a food processor and blitz together until well combined. Using a pestle and mortar, pound the cumin and coriander seeds until finely ground. Add to the processor (reserving a pinch to garnish) with the lemon zest and juice, 1 teaspoon salt and about 3 tablespoons olive oil. Blitz again until really smooth. If it is still quite stiff, add more olive oil and blitz until you have a soft, smooth purée. Season to taste.

Serve in a bowl with the reserved chickpeas, spices and parsley sprinkled over the top and some olive oil drizzled over.

baba ghanoush

2 aubergines/eggplants

2 garlic cloves, peeled

4 tablespoons tahini

3 tablespoons lemon juice

½ teaspoon sea salt

generous pinch of sweet smoked paprika

2 tablespoons extra virgin olive oil

1 tablespoon pomegranate seeds

Light 2 of the rings of your gas hob/burner on the lowest setting. Pierce the flesh of the aubergines/eggplants once or twice and place directly onto the flame. Char the skin all over, turning now and again. Let cool completely.

Carefully peel away all the skin. Keep any juice that comes out, as it contains a lot of flavour. Put aubergine/eggplant flesh, garlic, tahini, lemon juice, salt, paprika and olive oil in a food processor. Blitz until smooth. Serve in a bowl with a little more olive oil drizzled over and slightly stirred through, and the pomegranate seeds sprinkled over the top.

borlotti bean purée

250 g/1⅔ cups dried borlotti beans

400 ml/1⅔ cups extra virgin olive oil

2 tablespoons red wine vinegar

5 garlic cloves, peeled

a few sprigs fresh rosemary

handful of baby plum tomatoes

sea salt

Put the beans a bowl and cover with 3 times their volume of water. Allow to soak overnight.

The next day, refresh the beans in clean water and place in a large ovenproof pot. Bring almost to the boil, then cover and reduce to a gentle simmer for about 1 hour or until they are almost tender but not completely soft.

Preheat the oven to 200°C (400°F) Gas 6.

Drain most of the water, leaving about 100 ml/½ cup at the bottom, add the remaining ingredients and 1 teaspoon salt. Bake in the preheated oven for 30 minutes. Remove from the oven and let cool. Pull the leaves of the rosemary off the stalk, discard the stalk and put the leaves back in the pot. Bash everything with a potato masher until roughly mashed up with the oil.

This makes a delicious lunch during pumpkin season, served with a big bowl of salad and a cup of non-dairy yogurt. It's important to roll the dough really thinly to get snails that are slightly crunchy but melt in your mouth.

pastry snails with spicy pumpkin filling

MAKES 8

180 g/1⅓ cups unbleached plain/all-purpose flour

¼ teaspoon salt

3 tablespoons sunflower oil

For the filling

200 g/2 cups grated pumpkin, such as Hokkaido or other dense-fleshed pumpkin

½ onion, finely chopped

½ teaspoon tamari soy sauce

2 garlic cloves, crushed

¼ teaspoon salt

1 tablespoon olive oil, plus extra for brushing

½ teaspoon ground ginger

1 teaspoon lemon juice

freshly ground black pepper

baking sheet lined with parchment paper

Preheat the oven to 180°C (350°F) Gas 4.

Mix together the flour and salt, then add the oil and rub it in. Slowly add cold water (up to 80 ml/⅓ cup) to get a dough that doesn't stick to the work surface when you try to knead it.

Wrap the dough in clingfilm/plastic wrap and allow to rest at room temperature while you prepare the filling.

For the filling, mix together all the ingredients with your hands or a wooden spoon. Divide it into 8 equal portions.

Divide the dough into 4 equal portions. While you are working with one, keep the others wrapped in clingfilm/plastic wrap to prevent them drying out.

Put one portion of dough on a sheet of parchment paper, dust with a little flour and shape the dough into a small log with your hands. Roll it out with a rolling pin, as thinly as you can, into a square. The sheet of dough should be almost see-through. Trim any uneven edges, then cut in half to make 2 equal rectangles. These will make 2 snails.

Spread one portion of filling along the bottom edge of the rectangle. Roll the rectangle up carefully around the filling and into a nice, tight sausage. Bend it into a spiral/snail shape. Seal the edge by wetting your finger and pressing it gently but firmly against the snail. Tuck the end neatly underneath the snail.

Repeat with the remaining sheets and filling to get 8 snails.

Arrange the snails on the prepared baking sheet and brush them lightly with oil. Bake in the preheated oven for 35–40 minutes, or until golden.

Allow to cool slightly (or completely), then serve plain or brushed with a little more oil and soy sauce if you prefer them to be saltier. These snails are great as a portable meal too – very practical!

Fresh, crunchy, but also quite filling, these little canapés won't pass unnoticed! It is best to serve these canapés immediately, since the saltiness of the spread might make the courgette/zucchini wilt and let out its moisture.

courgette and walnut canapés

MAKES 20

140 g/1 cup chopped walnuts

2 tablespoons freshly chopped flat-leaf parsley

4 dried tomato halves, soaked, drained and chopped

½ teaspoon sweet paprika

⅛ teaspoon chilli powder

juice of ½ lemon

a little almond milk or water

1 medium courgette/zucchini, sliced diagonally into 3-mm/⅛-in. slices

30 g/½ cup alfalfa, chia and radish or other seed sprouts

sea salt

Blend all the ingredients (except the liquid, initially, courgette/zucchini and the seed sprouts) in a food processor or blender into a thick paste, seasoning with salt to taste. You're looking for a dense consistency that will spread and safely stay on a courgette/zucchini slice, but add a little almond milk or water if it's too thick. Taste and add more seasoning, if needed.

Gently pat the courgette/zucchini slices with paper towels if they're moist. Top with 1–2 teaspoons of the spread and garnish with some seed sprouts. Continue until you use up all the courgette/zucchini slices. Serve immediately. Depending on how much spread you used for each canapé, you might have some left over. This spread will keep in the refrigerator for a couple of days, so don't worry.

These savoury tarts are super-easy to make. You can put single servings of a delicious dip into these and have them as a contained and neat party snack. Think of these party tartlets as an elevated way to serve hummus and crackers.

party tartlets with hummus

MAKES 12–14

2 tablespoons ground flaxseeds/linseeds

170 g/1½ cups ground almonds/almond meal

a pinch of salt

2 tablespoons nutritional yeast

1½ teaspoons baking powder

dried oregano, to serve

For the hummus filling

400-g/14-oz. can of chickpeas, drained

freshly squeezed juice of 1 lemon

2 tablespoons tahini paste

1 tablespoon olive oil

sea salt and freshly ground black pepper

12 tartlet moulds

Preheat the oven to 180°C (350°F) Gas 4.

Put the flaxseeds/linseeds and 6 tablespoons water in a small bowl. Whisk the seeds into the water with a fork until the mixture starts to feel like the consistency of a beaten egg – in fact, what you have are 2 'flax eggs' that play the same role as eggs in plant-based baking recipes. Place in the refrigerator.

Put the ground almonds/almond meal, salt, nutritional yeast and baking powder in a food processor. Blitz together. At the last minute, add the 'flax egg' and blitz again until the 'flax egg' has been well incorporated – you don't want to overmix this. You should see a ball of dough start to form. Remove the dough from the processor and divide it into 12. Press each portion into a tartlet mould so that it neatly lines the base and sides of the mould. Trim off any excess dough with a sharp knife.

Put the tartlet moulds on a baking sheet in the middle of the preheated oven and bake for about 15 minutes, until you see the edges of the tartlets start to brown. Allow the tartlet cases to cool for a few minutes, at which point they should pop right out of the moulds.

To make the hummus filling, blitz all the ingredients together in a food processor until smooth.

Fill each tartlet case with a generous tablespoon of hummus and sprinkle a little oregano over the top.

These small, delicate bites are a real treat, not only because of their fresh taste but also because the bright red and light green combination of colours really gets noticed! Serve as an appetizer or amuse-bouche to impress your guests.

cherry tomatoes filled with spinach pesto

MAKES 20

20 cherry tomatoes
2 handfuls of baby spinach
85 g/⅔ cup sunflower seeds
4 tablespoons olive oil
2 garlic cloves, peeled
1 teaspoon lemon juice (to prevent oxidation of greens)
sea salt

Wash the tomatoes and remove their stems. Next, cut a very thin layer off the bottom of each tomato so that they can sit on a serving plate without rolling. Slice off the tops and scoop out the flesh with a small spoon to make enough space for the filling. Do this carefully so as not to damage the tomatoes.

Wash and drain the spinach well. Lightly dry-roast the sunflower seeds to release their full aroma. Place all the ingredients (except the tomatoes) in a blender and blend until smooth. Add 1–2 tablespoons water if necessary; the pesto should be liquid enough to be easily spooned or piped into the cored cherry tomatoes.

Fill each tomato carefully and serve immediately on fresh lettuce and seed sprouts, if desired.

If in season, use wild garlic (bear's garlic) instead of spinach for a beautiful aroma and an even more fluorescent green colour! Other soft greens and herbs work well, too. Also, you can use almonds, pine nuts, hazelnuts, sesame seeds, cashews or any other nuts and seeds instead of sunflower seeds to make this pesto.

Sushi is well known as a healthy choice. However, many Japanese restaurants only offer traditional sushi rolls, made with white sushi rice (usually prepared with white sugar). Until the day we can get a healthier fix for sushi and sushi rolls on the high street, here are some quinoa maki to satisfy that craving. This is a great way to use up quinoa or other grain leftovers from last night's dinner.

quinoa maki

MAKES 8

80 g/¾ cup cooked quinoa

2 teaspoons rice vinegar

4 sheets of sushi nori, about 20 x 20 cm/8 x 8 in.

2 carrots

10-cm/4-in. piece of cucumber

½ avocado

2–3 spring onions/scallions

handful of beansprouts

handful of microgreens, such as mizuna, pea shoots or watercress (optional)

1 teaspoon black or white sesame seeds

3 tablespoons tamari soy sauce

wasabi, to serve (optional)

pickled ginger, to serve (optional)

Put the quinoa and rice vinegar in a bowl and toss to coat.

Cut the nori sheets in half diagonally so that you have 8 triangular pieces. Cut the carrots and cucumber into matchsticks. Cut the avocado in half and make fine slices into the flesh, then peel off the skin. Chop the spring onions/scallions.

Take one nori triangle and spoon 1 tablespoon of the quinoa in a line along one of the short sides of the triangle. Place a few carrot and cucumber matchsticks on top, 2 or 3 slices of the avocado, a few beansprouts and microgreens, if using, and some spring onions/scallions. Try to put a greater portion of the vegetables towards what will be the larger end of your sushi cone. Roll the nori up all around the filling, then scatter a few sesame seeds at the mouth of the cone. Repeat with the rest of the nori pieces.

Serve with soy sauce, wasabi and pickled ginger, if using.

Along with the creamy avocado and sweet mango, these rolls are packed with three ingredients with high nutritional value: watercress, coriander/cilantro and alfalfa sprouts. Watercress is up there with kale, boasting a perfect score of 1000 on the ANDI scale (Aggregate Nutrient Density Index). Coriander/cilantro is one of the few foods that helps chelate heavy metals out of the body (such as mercury, lead and aluminium, which we accumulate through pollution, water and everyday products). And sprouts should be regarded a food group all of their own because they contain up to 100 times the enzymes that regular fruits and veggies do, as well as several times the protein and vitamin content. This really is a super-healthy snack!

mango-avocado summer rolls with lime dipping sauce

MAKES 6

6 rice paper wrappers

1 soft avocado, stoned/pitted and cut into slivers

2 mangoes, stoned and cut into slivers

small handful of alfalfa sprouts

3 large tablespoons coriander/cilantro leaves

handful of pea shoots

handful of mixed salad leaves such as watercress

small handful of cashews (optional)

1 lime

For the lime dipping sauce

1 lime

2–3 tablespoons tamari soy sauce

1 tablespoon balsamic vinegar

Fill a large bowl with warm water and place a rice paper wrapper in the bowl to soak and soften for about 1 minute. Soak the sheets one by one, otherwise they will stick together as they soften.

Remove the rice paper from the bowl and place it onto a kitchen towel to soak up the excess water. (Meanwhile, put a second wrapper in the bowl of warm water to soften.) Spoon one-sixth of the avocado, mango, sprouts, coriander/cilantro, pea shoots, salad leaves and cashews, if using, onto one half of the sheet in a neat column. Squeeze some lime juice over the filling. Fold the sides of the sheet up onto the filling, then tightly roll up the sheet over the filling to make a compact roll. Set aside and repeat this whole process with the remaining rice paper wrappers and filling.

For the lime dipping sauce, mix together the lime juice, soy sauce and balsamic vinegar in a small dish.

To serve, cut each roll in half on the diagonal and dip into a little bowl of the lime dipping sauce.

Eschew refined wheat and wrap your lunch in slightly-sweet and nutrient-dense chard instead. Try the filling here, or the Nectarine-tomato Salsa on page 18.

chard and cabbage wraps with peanut sauce

MAKES 4 LARGE WRAPS

4 large chard leaves (regular chard or rainbow chard, which has a red or orange stem)

½ head of white or red cabbage, or ¼ of each, finely chopped

2 carrots, grated

1 orange, halved

4 tablespoons sunflower seeds

1 tablespoon tamari soy sauce

For the peanut sauce

4 tablespoons peanut butter

1 garlic clove, crushed

1 teaspoon grated ginger (or you can use ground ginger in a pinch)

2 tablespoons sesame oil

2 tablespoons red wine vinegar

freshly squeezed juice of 1 lime

½–1 teaspoon chilli/chili powder (optional)

Wash the chard and dry thoroughly with some paper towels. Place each leaf face down on a board. If you can, carefully shave off the part of the stem that runs up the middle of the leaf and make small incisions along it – this will make the leaf easier to bend and roll.

Put the cabbage and carrots in a large bowl. Cut 1 orange half into small sections and squeeze the juice from the remaining half into the bowl.

Add the orange sections too.

Put the sunflower seeds in a non-stick frying pan/skillet over medium heat and toss occasionally. Dry-fry until they have browned slightly. This step is not crucial if you're in a hurry, but it does give the wraps the most unique flavour. Add the sunflower seeds and soy sauce to the bowl and stir well.

Place a quarter of the filling at one end of a chard leaf. Cut off the white stem if it is too long. Fold the sides of the leaf up onto the filling, then roll up the leaf over the filling to make a roll.

For the peanut sauce, put all the ingredients in a small dish and stir with a fork.

To serve, cut each roll in half on the diagonal and either dip them into the peanut sauce, or drizzle the sauce into the mouth of the wraps with a spoon.

These tasty, herb-rich roll-ups are one of the best ways to satisfy that craving for Italian food, without having to compromise your healthy intentions.

aubergine and courgette roll-ups

MAKES 12–14

2 large courgettes/zucchini

1 large aubergine/eggplant

4 teaspoons extra virgin olive oil

1 teaspoon dried thyme

75 g/¾ cup pine nuts

2 tablespoons nutritional yeast

1 tablespoon tomato purée/paste

5–6 sun-dried tomatoes

1 tablespoon dried rosemary

1 teaspoon dried marjoram

½ teaspoon sea salt

freshly ground black pepper

handful of fresh basil leaves

3–4 tablespoons shelled hemp seeds

baking sheet lined with foil
cocktail sticks/toothpicks
(optional)

Preheat the grill/broiler to medium.

Cut the courgettes/zucchini and aubergine/eggplant lengthways into long strips about 1 cm/½ inch thick. Arrange them on the prepared baking sheets and lightly brush the aubergine/eggplant with 1 teaspoon of the olive oil. Scatter the thyme over the vegetables. Grill/broil for about 3 minutes, then flip them over and grill/broil for another 3 minutes. Watch them carefully so that they don't burn. You may have to remove the courgettes/zucchini at this point and leave the aubergine/eggplant in for another 1–2 minutes. Once done, set them aside to cool.

Put the remaining olive oil, pine nuts, 5 tablespoons water, nutritional yeast, tomato paste, sun-dried tomatoes, rosemary, marjoram, salt and pepper in a food processor, and blitz until very smooth.

Take one vegetable strip, gently spread a thin layer of the mixture over it, lay some basil leaves on top and sprinkle with hemp seeds. Roll up the strip and spear with a cocktail stick/toothpick, if necessary, to seal it closed.

A salad for lunch can make you feel light and energized for the afternoon ahead. However, it can get boring to eat a bowl's worth of fresh veggies in the same bowl, with the same knife and fork day in, day out. Try using Baby Gem hearts as wraps and put the salad ingredients inside in. Don't just eat these for lunch – they also make a great appetizer for an informal party or dinner party.

baby gem lettuce wraps with sweet chilli sauce

MAKES 10–11

2 heads of Baby Gem lettuce

handful of fresh coriander/cilantro

2–3 spring onions/scallions

2 large carrots

1 pomegranate

For the sweet chilli sauce

1–2 fresh chillies/chiles, to taste (2 chillies/chiles will be very spicy)

1 garlic clove, crushed

½ teaspoon onion powder

125 ml/½ cup rice vinegar

2 heaped teaspoons stevia

½ teaspoon sea salt

1 tablespoon cornflour/cornstarch

coffee grinder or spice grinder (optional)

Tear the larger, outside leaves off the Baby Gem lettuce – these will become your wraps. Wash thoroughly and arrange on a plate.

To assemble the filling, cut the remaining lettuce as finely as you can so that it almost takes on a shredded texture. Do the same with the coriander/cilantro and spring onions/scallions, and place all three in a large bowl. Using a vegetable peeler, peel the carrots into ribbons and add to the bowl.

For the pomegranate, the best way to remove the seeds (or arils, to use their technical name) is to cut the fruit in half and place it in a large bowl of cold water. Then tear the flesh and separate the seeds by hand. You'll see that the seeds sink to the bottom of the bowl, whereas the white flesh floats. Next, pour away the water and flesh so that you just have the seeds left.

Add the seeds to the bowl of vegetables and mix well. Using a small spoon, fill the lettuce wraps with the mixture, making sure they're not too full to hold together.

To make the sweet chilli sauce, using a coffee or spice grinder, grind the chillies to a paste. If you don't have one of these, slice the chillies as thinly as possible. For a spicy sauce, include the seeds, otherwise omit them. Put the chillies, garlic, onion powder, rice vinegar, 125 ml/½ cup water, the stevia and salt in a saucepan over medium heat and bring to the boil. Allow the mixture to simmer until it has reduced down; about 8–10 minutes. Meanwhile, put the cornflour/cornstarch and 2 tablespoons water in a small bowl or cup, and stir until combined. Turn the chilli mixture down to low heat and add the cornflour/cornstarch mixture. Stir slowly for a couple of minutes until the sauce has thickened.

To serve, eat the lettuce wraps by hand, dipping them into the sweet chilli sauce as you go!

cookies
and bars

This recipe is great for getting children involved – they can help with rolling the cookie mixture into balls and pressing them flat on the baking sheet. They taste good – really good – and they never last for long.

peanut butter quinoa cookies

MAKES 24

420 g/1¾ cups smooth peanut butter

75 g/¾ cup xylitol or other sugar substitute

140 ml/¾ cup agave syrup

2 eggs (see Note)

1 teaspoon vanilla extract

45 g/½ cup quinoa flakes

2 tablespoons quinoa flour

½ teaspoon bicarbonate of soda/baking soda

baking sheet lined with parchment paper

Preheat the oven to 180°C (350°F) Gas 4.

Mix all ingredients together in a large mixing bowl. Once the ingredients are all combined, bring the mixture together in your hands, then roll into 2.5-cm/1-in. balls and place on the prepared baking sheet. Using your thumb, press down each ball so it is slightly flattened out.

Bake in the preheated oven for approximately 12 minutes, or until the cookies are golden, and serve warm. Store the cookies in an airtight container for up to 3 days.

Note: If you prefer not to use eggs you could use egg replacer or make a flax-egg mix by combining 2 tablespoons of ground flaxseeds/linseeds with 6 tablespoons of water.

Full of cocoa flavour and not overly sweet, these cookies will satisfy your chocolate craving the minute you bite into one! Make them a couple of times to see whether you prefer them soft and gooey or a little crispier.

gooey chocolate cookies

MAKES ABOUT 24

60 g/2¼ oz. dark/
   bittersweet chocolate,
   broken into pieces

65 g/⅓ cup sunflower oil

75 ml/⅓ cup soya/soy milk

200 g/¾ cup rice, maple or
   agave syrup

¼ teaspoon bourbon vanilla
   powder

130 g/1 cup unbleached
   plain/all-purpose flour

2 tablespoons unsweetened
   cocoa powder

¼ teaspoon ground
   cinnamon

¾ teaspoon baking powder

¼ teaspoon sea salt

*baking sheet lined with
   parchment paper*

Melt the chocolate in a heatproof bowl set over a pan of barely simmering water. Take care not to let the underside of the bowl touch the surface of the water. In a large mixing bowl, whisk the oil, milk, syrup and vanilla. Add the melted chocolate.

Preheat the oven to 180°C (350°F) Gas 4.

Place a sieve/strainer over the bowl containing the liquid ingredients (this way you won't need to use two separate bowls).

Put the flour, cocoa, cinnamon, baking powder and salt directly in the sieve/strainer and sift everything until it passes through the mesh. Use a spatula to incorporate all the ingredients into a smooth batter. It should not slide down the spoon – if it does, chill the batter in the refrigerator for 10 minutes.

Using a tablespoon, drop the batter onto the prepared baking sheet, 1 cm/⅜ in. apart. Bake for 12–14 minutes. The dough is dark to start with, so it's easy to burn them, and you want them still soft to the touch when you remove them from the oven. Check for doneness after 12 minutes, and bake them for no longer than 14 minutes.

Remove from the oven, slip the parchment paper with cookies onto the kitchen counter and let cool. Store in a cookie jar for a week or so.

These coconut-flavoured treats are a perfect Valentine's Day cookie. They are a unanimous crowd pleaser, though, so should be baked any day of the year.

chocolate-chip coconut cookies

MAKES 15–16

130 g/1 cup unbleached plain/all-purpose flour

60 g/¾ cup unsweetened desiccated/dried shredded coconut

1 teaspoon baking powder

½ teaspoon bicarbonate of soda/baking soda

½ teaspoon salt

60 ml/¼ cup coconut oil

100 ml/⅓ cup agave syrup

1 teaspoon vanilla extract

85 g/½ cup dark/bittersweet chocolate chips

baking sheet lined with foil

heart-shaped cookie cutter (optional)

Mix the flour, coconut, baking powder, bicarbonate of soda/baking soda and salt in a large bowl. You may want to sift the baking powder and bicarbonate of soda/baking soda with the flour first, since it's essential that these are evenly spread throughout your cookie dough before it goes in the oven.

Make sure the coconut oil is liquid. If it isn't, put it in a saucepan over low heat and allow to melt. Allow to cool completely, otherwise the hot oil will start to cook the other ingredients in the filling. Now make sure there's exactly 60 ml/¼ cup; sometimes it can be a little more or less than the initial quantity.

Mix the coconut oil, agave syrup and vanilla extract together. Bear in mind that they won't combine very easily because the oil and agave are very different consistencies, but do your best to give it a good stir.

Pour the wet mixture into the bowl of dry ingredients and mix with a wooden spoon. Add the chocolate chips. With your hands, compress the cookie dough into a ball, making sure the chocolate chips are incorporated.

Take 1 generous tablespoon of cookie dough into your hands at a time, compress it and roll it into a ball. You can either flatten the balls slightly on the prepared baking sheet to make round cookies, or you can press the ball of dough into the cookie cutter to mould it into a heart shape. Don't worry if the dough seems a little oily – this is normal. Bake the cookies in the preheated oven for about 10–12 minutes, or until they start to brown slightly. Remove the baking sheet from the oven and, using a spatula, transfer the cookies to a wire rack and allow to cool for at least 5 minutes before serving. Store in an airtight container for up to 3 days.

As healthy as oatmeal and raisins sound, the conventional versions of this popular cookie are far from it – they can be full of butter and refined sugar. This version is guilt-free, so you can enjoy it for breakfast, since it's full of health-giving ingredients.

oatmeal-raisin cookies

MAKES 16 MEDIUM AND 12 LARGE

1 tablespoon ground flaxseeds/linseeds

100 g/¾ cup brown rice flour or quinoa flour

1½ tablespoons baking powder

½ teaspoon ground cinnamon

½ teaspoon sea salt

120 g/1½ cups oats (rolled or whole/jumbo oats rather than the 'quick cook' versions)

60 ml/¼ cup coconut oil

60 ml/¼ cup pure maple syrup

½ teaspoon vanilla extract

100 g/¾ cup raisins

baking sheet lined with foil

Combine 1 tablespoon ground flaxseeds/linseeds with 3 tablespoons cold water. Mix well with a fork and refrigerate until needed.

In a mixing bowl, sift together the flour, baking powder, cinnamon and salt. Stir in the oats.

Gently melt the coconut oil in a small saucepan set over a gentle heat until completely liquid, then let cool. Stir in the maple syrup and vanilla extract. Remove the chilled flaxseed/linseed mixture from the refrigerator and mix it into the coconut and maple syrup mixture. Pour this wet mixture into the bowl of dry ingredients and incorporate well. Add the raisins and stir them in.

Spoon 2 heaped tablespoons of the mixture onto the prepared baking sheet at a time (or 3 for larger cookies), and press down gently with the back of the spoon to flatten. Bake the cookies in the preheated oven for about 12 minutes, until golden but still slightly soft.

Remove the cookies from the oven and allow them to cool for at least 10 minutes before eating, to allow them to firm up nicely. Store in an airtight container for up to 4 days.

This recipe is based on the popular doughy rolls filled with a sweet fig centre, known as Fig Newtons or fig rolls. The concept was based on an ancient Egyptian delicacy and popularized by American conglomerate Nabisco, who produced them in the flat cylindrical shape we know today.

Though the recipe may seem long and complicated, it's pretty foolproof, so if you've never baked before this is a great one to start with.

fig rolls

MAKES 35–40

For the crust

90 g/1 cup oats or oat flour

165 g/1½ cups ground almonds/almond meal

½ teaspoon sea salt

1 teaspoon baking powder

60 ml/¼ cup coconut oil

120 ml/½ cup agave syrup

60 ml/¼ cup unsweetened apple purée/applesauce

2 teaspoons pure vanilla extract

For the fig filling

150 g/1 cup dried figs, hard stems cut off

3 tablespoons freshly squeezed lemon juice

1 tablespoon agave syrup

¼ teaspoon ground ginger

baking sheet lined with parchment paper

food processor or blender

For the crust, if using oats, put them in a food processor and grind to a fine flour. Put the oat flour, ground almonds/almond meal, salt and baking powder in a bowl and mix.

Separately, combine the coconut oil, agave syrup, apple purée/applesauce and vanilla extract. Sift the dry ingredients into the bowl of wet ingredients and mix well. Refrigerate for at least 1 hour.

To make the fig filling, put the figs, lemon juice, agave syrup and ground ginger into the food processor or blender and pulse until a smooth paste forms. If your mixture isn't moving, gradually drizzle in up to 1 tablespoon water as needed.

Once your dough has properly chilled, preheat the oven to 180°C (350°F) Gas 4.

Divide the dough into 4. Take one portion and place it between 2 sheets of parchment paper. Using a rolling pin, roll it out into a rectangle about 25 x 10 cm/10 x 4 inches. Spread one quarter of the fig filling along one long edge of the dough rectangle, leaving a little border around it. Fold the bare half of the rectangle over onto the filling, then seal the ends of the rectangle by pressing the dough together with your fingers.

Repeat this process with the remaining portions of dough and filling. Arrange the dough cylinders on the prepared baking sheet. Bake in the preheated oven for about 12–14 minutes, or until the outside is slightly browned. Allow to cool completely, then cut into fat slices. Store in an airtight container for up to 5 days.

Keep a stash of these bars in your refrigerator, neatly wrapped up and ready to go! They are amazing for breakfast, as a pick-me-up snack or a guilt-free dessert. You can use millet flakes to make these bars gluten-free and any other dried fruits instead of apricots. Also, try adding orange juice and zest instead of lemon for the popular cocoa-orange combo.

pure energy bars

MAKES 8

2 very ripe bananas

3 tablespoons extra virgin coconut oil

grated zest of 1 organic lemon plus 1 tablespoon freshly squeezed lemon juice

15 unsulphured dried apricots, diced

200 g/2¼ cups fine rolled oats

¼ teaspoon ground cinnamon

⅛ teaspoon bourbon vanilla powder

3 tablespoons unsweetened cocoa powder

pinch of sea salt

18 x 18-cm/7 x 7-in. shallow dish or baking pan lined with clingfilm/plastic wrap

Peel the bananas and put them in a deep plate before mashing them thoroughly with a fork. If the coconut oil has solidified, set the jar in a bowl of boiling water until the oil begins to liquefy. Add the oil, lemon zest and juice and apricots to the mashed bananas and stir well. In a large bowl, combine the rolled oats, cinnamon, vanilla, cocoa and salt. Mix and add the banana mash to the dry ingredients. Use a spatula to combine the ingredients really well – there should be no dry patches of oats and the dough should be thick and sticky.

Place the dough in the prepared dish or pan and use a spatula or your hands to press it down until you get an even layer about 1.5 cm/½ in. thick. Wrap well with more clingfilm/plastic wrap and refrigerate for at least 2 hours (but best if left overnight). Unwrap the clingfilm/plastic wrap and cut into 8 even bars; wrap each one separately and use up during the week!

These homemade protein bars take less than 5 minutes to prepare and can be kept in your freezer for up to 3 weeks at a time, so that you never need to be stuck for a protein-rich snack.

on-the-go snack bars

MAKES 4

2 scoops protein powder of choice

60 ml/¼ cup canned unsweetened puréed pumpkin

60 ml/¼ cup almond butter (drain off the oil before measuring)

xylitol or stevia, to taste (optional)

6 tablespoons buckwheat groats

baking dish, about 23 x 10 cm/ 9 x 4 in., lightly greased with coconut oil

Put the protein powder, pumpkin and almond butter in a bowl and mix to combine. Add sweetener to taste – the protein powder and pumpkin make it plenty sweet enough on its own, but adjust it so that it tastes good to you. Stir in the buckwheat groats.

Spoon the mixture into the prepared baking dish, level it out with the back of a spoon and freeze for at least 1 hour.

Just to show you that you can match the commercial bars for protein with all-natural ingredients, check out these stats per bar (based on 1 bar being 16 g):

Protein powder: 8 g

Almond butter: 2.5 g

Buckwheat groats: 3 g

Pumpkin: 0.75 g

= more than 14 g total protein per bar

MAKES ABOUT 16

For the bottom layer

1 tablespoon ground
    flaxseeds/linseeds

3 tablespoons water

110 g/½ cup non-
    hydrogenated sunflower
    spread

110 g/2 cups plain corn flakes,
    with no added sugar

30 g/⅓ cup unsweetened
    cocoa powder

less than 45 g/¼ cup xylitol

75 g/1 cup unsweetened
    desiccated coconut

For the middle layer

110 g/½ cup non-
    hydrogenated sunflower
    spread

300 g/2 cups coconut palm
    sugar

2 teaspoons xanthan gum

1 tablespoon arrowroot

1 tablespoon maca powder
    (or gluten-free plain/all
    purpose flour of choice)

large handful of goji berries

½ teaspoon vanilla extract

2 tablespoons cherry juice or
    lemon juice, for tartness

For the top layer

175 g/1 cup dark/bittersweet
    chocolate chips, or
    coarsely chopped
    dark/bittersweet chocolate

180 ml/¾ cup almond milk

handful of walnuts, chopped

20- or 23-cm/8- or 9-in.
    square baking pan, lined
    with parchment paper

food processor or blender

Nanaimo bars are three-layer bars named after the town in
Canada where they originated. If you stick closely to the original
recipe you make the middle layer with custard but here we're
using vegan substitutes with the addition of goji berries.

walnut-goji nanaimo bars

For the bottom layer, put the flaxseeds/linseeds and 3 tablespoons water in
a small bowl. Whisk the seeds into the water with a fork until the mixture
starts to feel like the consistency of a beaten egg – in fact, what you have is
a 'flax egg' that plays the same role as an egg in plant-based baking recipes.
Place in the refrigerator.

Meanwhile, put the sunflower spread in a heatproof bowl over a pan
of barely simmering water and allow to melt. Put the corn flakes in a food
processor and pulse until they have formed a coarse meal – it should be
crunchy without any obvious corn-flake pieces. Once the sunflower spread
has melted, stir in the cocoa powder and xylitol. Remove from the heat and
stir in the ground corn flakes, desiccated coconut and 'flax egg'. Tip into
the prepared baking pan and press it down. Use the back of a big spoon
to smooth it level. Refrigerate while you prepare the middle layer.

For the middle layer, cream together the sunflower spread and coconut
sugar with a handheld electric whisk until pale. Add the xanthan gum,
arrowroot and maca powder and whisk again – the mixture will start to
thicken up. Stir in the goji berries, vanilla extract and juice. Remove the pan
from the freezer and spread this middle layer evenly over the bottom layer.
Freeze again.

For the top layer, put the chocolate and almond milk in a heatproof bowl
over a saucepan of barely simmering water. Leave until melted and
completely smooth.

Remove the pan from the freezer and spread the melted chocolate
mixture on top. Press the walnuts into the surface of the chocolate.
Freeze again until totally hardened – about 45 minutes.

To serve, cut into 5-cm/2-inch squares and serve cold.

Spirulina is possibly the least palatable of the superfoods. It's a very powerful alkalizer, and alkalizing foods help bring the body to its 'happy place' where it can function at its best. These energy bites are a delicious way to introduce spirulina to your diet.

coconut and spirulina energy bites

MAKES ABOUT 16

90 g/½ cup dates, stoned/pitted

65 g/½ cup cashews

1 large teaspoon coconut oil

1½–2 teaspoons spirulina powder

1 heaped teaspoon matcha powder (green tea powder)

about 20 g/¼ cup unsweetened desiccated/ dried shredded coconut

food processor or blender

Soak the dates in a bowl of water for 30 minutes, but no longer than that.

Put the cashews in a food processor fitted with an 'S' blade and pulse for about 30–45 seconds until a thick meal has formed.

Rinse the dates, wipe off any extra moisture and add them to the food processor along with the coconut oil, spirulina and matcha powder. Process until a large ball starts to form. Remove the blade and take the processor bowl off the stand.

Using a small cup half-filled with water to wet your hands as you go, pinch off pieces of the mixture about the size of whole walnuts. Roll them into balls between the palms of your hands. (Damp hands will stop the mixture sticking too much.)

Roll each ball in the desiccated coconut to coat it evenly, then place on a plate or board. Repeat with the rest of the mixture.

Refrigerate the energy bites for at least 20 minutes. Store in the refrigerator in an airtight container for up to 3 weeks.

Flapjack recipes often somehow manage to defeat the purpose of the healthy oats by drowning them in sugar. Try this sugar-free version of the well-known flapjacks, which are just as delicious and chewy, while still being good for you.

flapjacks

SERVES 10–12

100 g/6½ tablespoons coconut oil

20 g/4 teaspoons sunflower spread

130 ml/½ cup sunflower oil

2 ripe bananas, mashed

2 teaspoons pure vanilla extract

140 g/¾ cup xylitol or coconut palm sugar

60 ml/¼ cup agave syrup

1 tablespoon date syrup

a good pinch of sea salt

500 g/4 cups rolled oats

150 g/1 cup raisins

100 g/¾ cup pumpkin seeds

60 g/½ cup pecans

100 g/⅔ cup unsulphured dried apricots, chopped

*baking pan, about
    20–25 cm/8–10 in.*

Preheat the oven to 180°C (350°F) Gas 4.

Gently heat the coconut oil, sunflower spread, sunflower oil, bananas, vanilla extract, xylitol or coconut sugar, agave syrup, date syrup and salt in a saucepan just until the sunflower spread has melted. Whisk the mixture together until smooth.

In a large mixing bowl, combine the oats, raisins, pumpkin seeds, pecans and apricots. Add the molten mixture from the pan and mix very well. Spoon the mixture into the baking pan and flatten it out. Bake in the preheated oven for about 25 minutes, or until the flapjacks are a lovely golden, light brown colour. If it looks like they are colouring too quickly, turn the heat down to 160°C (325°F) Gas 3. The main thing is not to burn the top, as the raisins and apricots burn easily and become very bitter.

With flapjacks, you really can make them your own. If you are less keen on the dried fruit, take it out or add some other nuts or seeds.

Honestly, who doesn't love a good sticky and chewy chocolate brownie? They are the ultimate in decadent home baking – rich and moist and totally addictive. This recipe is completely sin free, yet still delicious and indulgent-tasting. People will beg you for the recipe when they find out they are sugar, wheat and dairy free.

orange-zest brownies

SERVES 10–12

225 g/7½ oz. dark/ bittersweet chocolate, at least 70% cocoa solids, chopped

110 g/1 cup rice flour

70 g/½ cup plus 1 tablespoon unsweetened cocoa powder

½ teaspoon baking powder

½ teaspoon sea salt

225 g/7 oz. dairy-free butter, e.g. sunflower or soy spread

170 g/¾ cup coconut palm sugar or xylitol

2 eggs

2 egg yolks

grated zest of 1 orange

100 g/⅔ cup pecans, lightly roasted

small baking pan or roasting pan, lined with parchment paper

Preheat the oven to 180°C (350°F) Gas 4.

Melt the chocolate in a heatproof bowl over a saucepan of simmering water, making sure the base of the bowl does not touch the water.

Sift the flour, cocoa powder, baking powder and salt into a bowl. In another bowl, beat the butter with the sugar until pale and fluffy. Slowly mix in the eggs and egg yolks, then the melted chocolate and orange zest. Finally, stir in the sifted ingredients and pecans. As the melted chocolate cools, the mixture becomes increasingly stiff and difficult to mix, to the point that you may think you have made a mistake and need to add more liquid... but don't! This is what makes these brownies so decadently chewy and dense in texture. If you have a food mixer it makes the job a little easier, otherwise work those triceps!

Spoon the mixture into the prepared baking pan and, with the back of a metal spoon, level the top. Dipping the spoon into hot water every now and again prevents it from sticking. Bake in the preheated oven for 25–30 minutes, depending on your oven and the thickness of your brownie. A skewer should come out with a bit of the wet mixture still on it, as the brownie will firm up once it has cooled completely and the chocolate sets. Once cool, cut into small squares, as it is very rich. Then devour!

This is a recipe for the most indulgent, yet guilt-free truffles you will ever taste, using a few healthy alternatives. This may seem like a contradiction, but just taste one and you will understand.

chocolate truffles

MAKES 24–28

handful of pecans and hazelnuts

a pinch of sea salt

150 ml/⅔ cup soy cream/creamer

30 g/2 tablespoons coconut oil

200 g/6½ oz. unsweetened dark/bittersweet chocolate, at least 70% cocoa solids: 150 g/5 oz. of it grated, and the rest chopped

1 tablespoon xylitol or coconut palm sugar

grated zest of ½ orange

unsweetened cocoa powder, for rolling

1 teaspoon sunflower oil

2 skewers

Preheat the oven to 180°C (350°F) Gas 4.

Roast the nuts on a baking sheet in the preheated oven for 10 minutes, or until they have gone a shade darker. Allow to cool, then crush or finely chop with a pinch of salt.

Put the soy cream/creamer and coconut oil in a saucepan until hot and the coconut oil has melted but is not simmering. Add the grated chocolate, xylitol and a pinch of salt while stirring quickly with a whisk. Keep whisking until all the chocolate has melted and you have a smooth mixture. Transfer to a bowl, keeping a third aside. Mix this third with the orange zest. Allow them all to cool, then cover with clingfilm/plastic wrap and refrigerate for at least 4 hours or until more solid and pliable.

To shape the truffles, keep the mixture in the refrigerator if you can and try to handle it as little as possible, as the warmth of your hands will melt it. Coat your hands in cocoa powder. Take a teaspoonful of the mixture and quickly roll it between flat hands until you have a neat ball shape, then place on a plate in the refrigerator. Continue until you have used all the mixture, doing the same with the orange-zest mixture. Refrigerate for at least 1 hour.

To make chocolate-coated truffles, melt the chopped chocolate and sunflower oil in a heatproof bowl over a saucepan of simmering water, making sure the base of the bowl does not touch the water. Insert a skewer about 1 cm/½ in. into the base of one of the truffles, then dip it into the melted chocolate, quickly swirling it around to make sure it is completely covered. Using a second skewer, slide the truffle off the tip and onto a plate lined with parchment paper. Continue until you have coated half of the plain truffles. Once the chocolate has set, put the plate in the refrigerator until ready to serve.

Roll the remaining plain truffles between warm hands to soften the outside slightly, then roll in the nuts until completely covered and place in the refrigerator. Roll the orange-zest truffles in cocoa powder and shake off any excess. Refrigerate with the others.

Remove the truffles from the refrigerator about 10 minutes before you want to serve them. They keep well in the refrigerator but are best enjoyed as soon as possible, which won't be a problem!

Store-bought caramel is delicious. But it is made with white sugar boiled in water and then mixed with cream or butter, along with a host of additives and preservatives. So here's an even more delicious version of caramel with vitamin-rich dates and a touch of peanut butter.

chocolate-covered caramels

MAKES ABOUT 6

200 g/1 cup dates, stoned/pitted

1 tablespoon smooth peanut butter (unsweetened, made without any hydrogenated oils)

1 tablespoon coconut oil

a pinch of sea salt

250 g/9 oz. unsweetened dark/bittersweet chocolate, chopped

food processor or blender

freezer-proof baking sheet or plate lined with clingfilm/plastic wrap

Put the dates in a bowl of room-temperature water and allow them to soak for a few hours. They will soften and absorb some of the water, which will help when making the caramel.

Rinse the dates and put them in a food processor or blender. Blitz until smooth, scraping down the edges of the bowl as you go. Once the dates have started to form a paste, add the peanut butter and continue to pulse. Lastly, add the coconut oil for texture and the salt to bring out the flavour.

Process again until the mixture naturally forms a large ball.

Pull off bite-size pieces of the mixture with your fingers and roll them into neat balls. Lay them out on the prepared baking sheet and freeze for at least 30 minutes.

Meanwhile, put the chocolate in a heatproof bowl over a saucepan of barely simmering water. Do not let the base of the bowl touch the water. Leave until melted and completely smooth.

Remove the chilled caramel balls from the freezer. Place 1 caramel on a spoon and dip it into the melted chocolate so that it is completely and evenly coated. Return the ball to the prepared baking sheet. You can use 2 teaspoons to help shape the chocolate coating if that helps. Repeat with the remaining caramel balls, then freeze for at least 20 minutes to give the chocolate and caramel layers enough time to harden properly. Once they've frozen, you can transfer them to a freezer bag.

Remove the caramels from the freezer just before serving. Store them in the freezer for up to 2 weeks.

This is a spin on the classic American confectionery, Peanut Butter Cups. Almonds are rich in Vitamin E and contain less saturated fat than peanuts. This recipe uses nutritional yeast, which is a dried inactive yeast that gives the almond butter an amazing flavour kick. Much like brewer's yeast, nutritional yeast contains the complete profile of B vitamins, as well as being composed of 50% protein. You can of course leave this out if you choose, but it really does take things up a notch!

almond butter cups

MAKES 12 LARGE CUPS OR 24 MINI CUPS

215 ml/1 cup coconut oil

60 g/¾ cup unsweetened cocoa powder

4 tablespoons agave syrup

1 tablespoon stevia (or 2 more tablespoons agave syrup)

a dash of vanilla extract

4–5 tablespoons almond butter

1 teaspoon nutritional yeast

a pinch of sea salt (if using unsalted almond butter)

12-hole muffin pan, or 24-hole mini muffin pan, lined with paper cases

Put the coconut oil in a saucepan over low heat and allow to melt. Stir in the cocoa powder, agave syrup, stevia, if using, and vanilla extract until you have smooth liquid chocolate. Divide one third of the mixture between the muffin cases and put the whole muffin pan in the freezer until the mixture has solidified – about 5 minutes.

Meanwhile, mix the almond butter, nutritional yeast and salt, if needed, in a bowl.

Remove the muffin pan from the freezer and place a generous teaspoon of the almond-yeast mixture in the centre of each base of frozen chocolate, then flatten it slightly with your fingers. Pour the remaining melted chocolate over the almond-yeast mixture. Put the whole muffin pan in the freezer again until the mixture has solidified – about 10 minutes.

Remove the almond butter cups from the freezer just before serving to get them at their most firm and crisp. If you store them in the freezer or refrigerator, they will keep for 3–4 weeks (unless you devour them before!).

This is a frozen, chocolatey nut butter concoction, great for when you are really craving dark/bittersweet chocolate. It's very common for women to crave chocolate at certain points in their cycles: what they're actually lacking is a hit of magnesium, which helps regulate the nervous system and aids sleep too. If you can find raw cocoa powder, use it in this recipe as its potency is greater than that of regular cocoa powder.

cocoa-almond freezer fudge pops

MAKES 8

70 ml/¼ cup almond butter (drain off the oil before measuring)

2 teaspoons ground flaxseeds/linseeds

1 large teaspoon coconut oil

1 large teaspoon xylitol

1½ tablespoons unsweetened cocoa powder, plus extra for dusting

½ teaspoon pure vanilla extract

for an extra boost, add 1 teaspoon espresso powder

food processor or blender

Put all the ingredients in a food processor or blender and blitz until smooth.

Divide the mixture into 8 and roll each portion into a ball between the palms of your hands. Dust in cocoa powder.

Freeze the fudge pops for at least 30 minutes and consume straight from the freezer. Store in the freezer for up to 4 weeks.

This recipe for cookie dough balls is inspired by the store-bought sweet logs that you can either eat straight up or shape into cookies and cook. Here, the baking powder and sugar have been omitted as these babies don't go anywhere near an oven!

frozen cookie dough balls

MAKES 18–24

60 g/⅓ cup xylitol

75 g/⅓ cup non-hydrogenated sunflower spread, at room temperature

about 120 g/¾ cup wholemeal/whole-wheat gluten-free plain/all-purpose flour

1½ teaspoons vanilla extract

½ teaspoon sea salt

175 g/1 cup dark/bittersweet chocolate chips, or coarsely chopped dark/bittersweet chocolate

freezer-proof baking sheet or plate, lined with clingfilm/plastic wrap

Put the xylitol in a high-speed blender and blend until you a have a powdery, icing/confectioners' sugar-like substance.

Put the sunflower spread in a large bowl and mash with a fork. Add the flour and powdered xylitol and whisk slowly with a handheld electric whisk. With dry powders you want to make sure you're gentle to start with or they'll fly all over the place. Add the vanilla extract and salt once the mixture is smooth and whisk them in.

Finally, add the chocolate chips and stir to combine.

Pull off bite-size pieces of the dough with your fingers and roll them into neat balls. Lay them out on the prepared baking sheet and freeze for at least 30 minutes. Once they've frozen, you can transfer them to a freezer bag. Consume frozen.

cakes and muffins

It's always nice to have a vegan dessert recipe on hand. Sorghum is an ancient grain from the grass species that is commonly used as a gluten-free flour. It is a good base flour, since it pairs well with other flours and has little flavour. Freekeh flour is another ancient grain, now more often used as flour, that could be used here.

vegan chocolate fudge cake

SERVES 8

30 g/¼ cup sorghum flour

30 g/¼ cup teff flour

35 g/¼ cup potato starch

1½ teaspoons baking powder

½ teaspoon bicarbonate of soda/baking soda

½ teaspoon sea salt

3 tablespoons milled flaxseeds/linseeds

230 ml/1 cup coffee

100 ml/½ cup agave

100 g/½ cup xylitol or other sugar substitute

2 teaspoons lemon juice

60 g/⅔ cup cocoa powder

95 ml/½ cup vegetable oil

1 tablespoon vanilla extract

1 teaspoon xanthan gum

23-cm/9-in. cake pan, greased and dusted with almond flour

Preheat the oven to 180°C (350°F) Gas 4.

Sift the sorghum flour, teff flour and potato starch together in a large mixing bowl. Add the baking powder, bicarbonate of soda/baking soda and salt to the sifted flours and mix.

In a separate bowl, whisk the flaxseeds/linseeds together with the coffee. Add the remaining wet ingredients to the flax–coffee mix and stir together.

Add the dry mixture to the wet and whisk until fully combined. Pour into the prepared cake pan and bake in the preheated oven for 25 minutes until a knife comes out clean from the centre.

Serve immediately and enjoy.

Mesquite flour is made from grinding mesquite pods. It has a smoky, nutty and sweet flavour that pairs perfectly with cinnamon. You will fall in love with its unique aroma immediately and it's now readily available in health-food stores as a gluten-free alternative to wheat flour. It's best mixed with other flours because it has such a dominant flavour. You can add a scoop of this flour to your pancake batter too!

spice cake with mesquite flour

MAKES 16

3 egg whites and 2 egg yolks

140 g/1 cup potato starch

50 g/½ cup quinoa flour

65 g/½ cup teff flour

75 g/¾ cup mesquite flour

2 teaspoons xanthan gum

1 teaspoon bicarbonate of soda/baking soda

1½ teaspoons baking powder

½ teaspoon sea salt

3 teaspoons cinnamon

1 teaspoon nutmeg

¼ teaspoon ground cloves

150 ml/¾ cup vegetable oil

140 g/¾ cup xylitol or other sugar substitute

300 g/1¼ cups apple purée/applesauce

a 23-cm/9-in. cake pan lined with parchment paper

Preheat the oven to 180°C (350°F) Gas 4.

Beat the egg whites to soft peaks and set aside. Whisk all of the dry ingredients together. Then, in a separate bowl, beat the vegetable oil, xylitol, apple purée/applesauce and egg yolks together. Beat the wet and dry ingredients together to form a smooth batter. Then gently fold in the egg whites and softly whisk the mixture until completely mixed.

Pour the batter into the prepared cake pan. Bake in the preheated oven for 35 minutes, or until a metal skewer comes out clean from the centre. Leave to cool in the pan before turning out.

Naturally wheat free (it is made with ground almonds) and supremely moist, drowned in a sweet orange syrup, this exotic cake never fails to impress.

moroccan orange cake

SERVES 10–12

300 g/1½ cups ground almonds/amond meal

250 g/1⅓ cups xylitol

2 teaspoons baking powder

5 eggs

200 ml/generous ¾ cup sunflower oil

2 teaspoons agave syrup for the cake, plus 60 ml/ 5 tablespoons for the syrup

grated zest and freshly squeezed juice of 1 large orange

grated zest and freshly squeezed juice of ½ lemon

3 cloves

3 cinnamon sticks

soy yogurt with some ground cinnamon stirred though, to serve

20-cm/8-in. springform pan, base-lined with parchment paper

Preheat the oven to 180°C (350°F) Gas 4.

In a bowl, mix together the ground almonds/almond meal, xylitol and baking powder.

In a separate bowl, whisk together the eggs, sunflower oil, the 2 teaspoons of agave syrup and the orange and lemon zest. Pour the mixture into the dry ingredients and mix together.

Pour the cake mixture into the prepared baking pan and bake in the preheated oven for 35–45 minutes, or until a skewer inserted in the middle comes out clean. If the top looks like it is going to burn, cover it with foil, being careful not to press it on the cake. Allow to cool slightly while you make a syrup.

Put the orange and lemon juices, the 60 ml/5 tablespoons agave syrup, cloves and cinnamon in a saucepan. Bring to the boil, reduce the heat and simmer for 5 minutes.

While the cake is still warm, turn it out onto a plate, drizzle the syrup over and allow it to seep in. If it is not all absorbed at once, keep it aside to drizzle over later. When you are ready to serve, pile the cinnamon sticks and cloves on top of one another on the cake. Serve with the cinnamon-soy yogurt dolloped onto each slice.

This healthified banana cake is not only sugar-free but also dairy- and egg-free. It's the perfect family bake and can be enjoyed alongside a mid-morning cup of coffee with friends or as a supper-time treat for kids. This super-soft banana cake will keep for up to 3 days but is sure to be polished off in no time.

banana cake

SERVES ABOUT 14

3 teaspoons ground chia seeds (buy them ready ground, or grind whole seeds in a coffee/spice grinder)

2 very ripe bananas

250 g/1 cup plus 1 tablespoon non-dairy spread or coconut oil

340 g/2½ cups gluten-free plain/all-purpose flour of choice

3⅓ teaspoons baking powder

1 teaspoon sea salt

225 g/generous 1 cup xylitol

1 teaspoon pure vanilla extract

22–23-cm/9-in. bundt/ring pan (the hole in the middle should be about 10 cm/4 in. wide), or 23-cm/9-in. round cake pan, greased

Preheat the oven to 160°C (320°F) Gas 3.

Put the ground chia seeds in a small bowl with 3 tablespoons water. Whisk the seeds into the water with a fork until the mixture starts to feel like the consistency of a beaten egg – in fact, what you have are 3 'chia eggs' that play the same role as eggs in plant-based baking recipes. Place in the refrigerator.

Meanwhile, mash the bananas with a fork and set aside.

Put the spread or coconut oil in a saucepan over low heat and leave just until softened.

In a large bowl, sift together the flour, baking powder, salt and xylitol. Add the vanilla extract, chia mixture, and soft spread or coconut oil and stir well. Gently fold in the bananas.

Spoon the mixture into the prepared baking pan and bake in the preheated oven for 40 minutes. Reduce the temperature to 55°C/130°F or the lowest your oven will go. Bake for a further 20 minutes. Cover the cake with foil if it's looking brown on top but it's not baked all the way through yet.

Remove the cake from the oven and allow to cool for 15 minutes before serving. Store in an airtight container for up to 3 days.

If you are new to cake making and particularly to baking with healthy ingredients, this is a great recipe to wet your toes with. It's so easy to put together and there's very little possibility of error. This cake is especially good baked on a cosy autumnal afternoon and enjoyed in front of a warm open fire.

apple and cinnamon cake

SERVES ABOUT 14

240 g/2 cups gluten-free plain/all-purpose flour of choice

3½ teaspoons baking powder

1 teaspoon ground cinnamon

½ teaspoon sea salt

475 ml/2 cups unsweetened apple purée/applesauce

120 ml/½ cup agave syrup or pure maple syrup (maple syrup works particularly well here)

80 ml/⅓ cup rice milk

75 g/½ cup sultanas/golden raisins, raisins, or a mixture of both (or even chocolate chips, but the dried fruit goes particularly well with the apple-cinnamon flavours)

22–23-cm/9-in. bundt/ring pan (the hole in the middle should be about 10 cm/ 4 in. wide), 20-cm/8-in. square baking pan, or 23-cm/9-in. round cake pan

Preheat the oven 180°C (350°F) Gas 4.

Sift the flour and baking powder together into a bowl, then add the cinnamon and salt and mix by hand. Create a hole or a well in the centre of the ingredients – you will pour the wet mixture into this well later and this method will prevent too much lumpiness in the batter.

Separately, combine the apple purée/applesauce, agave syrup and rice milk. Pour this wet mixture, one third at a time, into the well in your bowl of dry ingredients. Stir as you go, preferably with a spatula but a wooden spoon will be fine too. Be sure not to overmix, and don't worry about a few lumps. Add the dried fruit and make sure it is well distributed throughout the mixture.

Spoon the mixture into the baking pan – it's a very wet mixture so you don't need to grease your pan. Bake in the middle of the preheated oven for 40 minutes, or until a cocktail stick/toothpick inserted into the middle of the cake comes out clean. Cover the cake with foil if it's looking brown on top but it's not baked all the way through yet. Allow the cake to cool for at least 10 minutes before cutting into it. Store in an airtight container for up to 3 days.

More like mini cakes than muffins, the spelt flour gives these a wonderfully chewy texture and the apples keep them nice and moist, so they taste just as good the next day... although if you are anything like me, you will have them all polished off in one sitting. These are great for breakfast, or to bring to work for an indulgent yet healthy snack. If you are coeliac, you can use rice flour.

apple, raisin and cinnamon muffins

MAKES 6 LARGE MUFFINS

1 cooking/tart apple, peeled, cored and diced

150 g/1 cup plus 2 tablespoons spelt flour

150 g/1¼ cups rolled oats

100 g/⅔ cup raisins

2 teaspoons baking powder

1 teaspoon bicarbonate of soda/baking soda

3 teaspoons ground cinnamon

1 teaspoon mixed/apple pie spice

¼ teaspoon grated nutmeg

a good pinch of sea salt

2 eggs, lightly beaten

125 ml/½ cup soy yogurt

1 eating/dessert apple, peeled, cored and diced

220 ml/1 scant cup pure maple syrup

6-hole muffin pan, greased or lined with muffin cases/liners or squares of parchment paper

Preheat the oven to 180°C (350°F) Gas 4.

Put the chopped cooking apple in a small saucepan with 3 tablespoons water. Bring to the boil, then simmer until completely soft. Mash with a fork and set aside to cool.

In a large bowl, stir together the spelt flour, oats, raisins, baking powder, bicarbonate of soda/baking soda, cinnamon, mixed/apple pie spice, nutmeg and salt. Add the eggs, yogurt, mashed cooking apple, maple syrup and chopped eating/dessert apple. Mix together.

Spoon the mixture into the prepared muffin pan. Bake in the preheated oven for about 30 minutes. A skewer should come out pretty much clean, but a tiny bit of the muffin mixture on the skewer is OK, as it will continue to cook a little while cooling, leaving you with a nice moist middle.

For an after-dinner treat, you can serve the muffins with soy yogurt mixed with a little maple syrup and ground cinnamon.

MAKES ABOUT 8

For the dough

2¼ teaspoons fast-action dried yeast

250 ml/1 cup warm (not hot) water

125 ml/½ cup agave syrup or pure maple syrup

360 g/3 cups gluten-free plain/all-purpose flour, plus extra for dusting

1 tablespoon ground cinnamon

1 tablespoon baking powder

1 teaspoon sea salt

½ teaspoon xanthan gum

175 ml/¾ cup coconut oil

1 teaspoon pure vanilla extract

2 tablespoons apple cider vinegar

For the filling

130 g/1 cup almonds

1 teaspoon ground cinnamon

75 g/½ cup coconut palm sugar, or other granulated sweetener of choice (coconut sugar gives the buns an earthy, caramel-y taste)

a few heaped tablespoons non-hydrogenated sunflower spread, for spreading

For the glaze

95 g/½ cup xylitol

2–3 tablespoons almond milk

round baking pan or Pyrex dish, 23-cm/9-in. diameter, greased

These are your new go-to bakes for special-occasion tea parties, long, lazy brunches and cosy weekends out of the cold.

cinnamon buns

For the dough, put the yeast and warm water in a bowl and mix. Mix in the agave or maple syrup and let sit. You will see foam start to form on the surface – this is good.

Put the flour, cinnamon, baking powder, salt and xanthan gum in a large bowl and mix with a balloon whisk to make sure everything is well incorporated. Mix the coconut oil, vanilla and vinegar into the yeast mixture. Now stir this into the bowl of dry ingredients with a wooden spoon. It will be very sticky and light, but that's normal. Cover lightly with clingfilm/plastic wrap, then a damp cloth, and allow to rise for 1 hour.

Uncover the dough and poke it: if it bounces back, it is ready. (If not, rest it a little longer.) Sprinkle flour over the dough and form it into a ball. It will be very stretchy, so add as much flour as needed. Freeze for 15 minutes.

For the filling, blitz the almonds, cinnamon and sugar in a food processor until crumbly.

Preheat the oven to 200°C (400°F) Gas 6.

Dust flour over a large surface and place the dough on top. Knead it well by stretching it away from itself with your palms and squashing it back together. Flour as you go along. Dust more flour on the surface and use a rolling pin to roll out the dough until it's roughly 40 x 25 cm/16 x 10 inches. Warm the sunflower spread between your fingers and spread it over the dough. Scatter the filling over it. Starting from a long edge, roll up the dough very tightly (as it will expand in the oven). Flour the outside of the dough if it's sticking to your surface. Once you have rolled almost all the way, fold the top end over the roll: this will make it easier to cut. Using a sharp knife, cut the roll into about 10-cm/4-inch slices. Arrange the slices, cut side down, in the prepared dish, leaving a little space between. Bake in the preheated oven for 22–25 minutes, or until a cocktail stick/toothpick inserted in the dough comes out clean.

For the glaze, blitz the xylitol in a high-speed blender until finely ground. Put in a bowl with 1 tablespoon of the milk. Stir and drizzle in milk until you reach a consistency you like. Remove the buns from the oven, allow to cool for 5 minutes, then drizzle the glaze over them. Store in an airtight container for up to 4 days.

There is a myth going around that Easter buns are very tricky to make and that you must be an experienced baker to get it right without adding a couple of eggs to the dough. Here's a simple, vegan Easter bun recipe that you can (and should) make throughout the year, not only for Easter!

sugar-free italian easter buns

MAKES 3 LARGE BUNS

sunflower oil, for brushing

For the starter

6 tablespoons plain soy milk, lukewarm

9 g/2 teaspoons dried/active dry yeast (additive-free)

25 g/2 tablespoons rice, pure maple or agave syrup

2 tablespoons strong unbleached bread flour

For the dough

40 g/⅓ cup unsulphured dried apricots, chopped

40 g/⅓ cup raisins

3 tablespoons rum

grated zest of 1 orange

500 g/4 cups strong unbleached bread flour or unbleached spelt flour

½ teaspoon sea salt

⅛ teaspoon ground turmeric

170 ml/¾ cup plain soy milk

100 g/¾ cup non-hydrogenated margarine

2 teaspoons pure vanilla extract

65 g/¼ cup rice, pure maple or agave syrup, plus extra for brushing

baking sheet lined with parchment paper

Mix together the starter ingredients in a mixing bowl, cover and allow to rest for 30 minutes or until doubled in size.

For the dough, mix together the apricots, raisins, rum and orange zest in a bowl and allow to soak while the starter is rising.

Sift together the flour, salt and turmeric in a bowl.

Heat the milk in a saucepan until hot, then add the margarine and stir until melted. Add the vanilla extract and syrup, then the soaked fruit as well as the starter. Mix well. Pour into the flour mixture and combine with a wooden spoon to get a smooth lump of dough. Transfer to a floured surface and knead vigorously for at least 5 minutes, until silky and elastic.

Place in an oiled bowl, cover with a wet kitchen towel and allow to rise in a warm spot for 2½ hours, or until doubled in size.

Punch down the dough, give it a quick knead, then divide it into three equal portions. Shape each into a ball and put on the prepared baking sheet. Snip V-shaped cuts into the top of each loaf so that they open up during baking. Cover well with a kitchen towel and allow to rise again for 30 minutes, or until doubled in size.

Preheat the oven to 200°C (400°F) Gas 6.

Brush a little oil over the buns and bake in the preheated oven for 30–60 minutes, or until golden. Brush syrup over them while still hot, then transfer to a wire rack to cool.

These should be stored wrapped in a kitchen towel in a cool and dry place and will keep for a week or a little longer.

MAKES 24

For the doughnuts

160 g/1⅓ cups gluten-free plain/all-purpose flour

½ teaspoon xanthan gum

65 g/⅓ cup xylitol

1½ teaspoons baking powder

1 teaspoon bicarbonate of soda/baking soda

1 teaspoon ground cinnamon

½ teaspoon sea salt

125 ml/½ cup almond or rice milk

2 tablespoons apple cider vinegar

1½ tablespoons sunflower oil

5 tablespoons unsweetened apple purée/applesauce

1 teaspoon vanilla extract

For the cinnamon 'sugar'

1 big serving spoon non-hydrogenated sunflower spread (about 60 ml/¼ cup, but it doesn't need to be precise)

2 teaspoons ground cinnamon

5 tablespoons xylitol or stevia

1 or 2 mini-doughnut pans (enough to make 24 doughnuts), greased with coconut oil or sunflower spread

disposable sandwich bag, or piping/pastry bag fitted with a plain nozzle/tip

It's pretty unanimous that a great doughnut is airy, moist and soft. When baking without a ton of eggs to help us with the fluffiness, it's essential to use both baking powder and bicarbonate of soda/baking soda to make the batter rise the way we want it to, and xanthan gum for texture. Once you have all your ingredients assembled, though, this an easy bake to make.

mini baked doughnuts with cinnamon 'sugar'

Preheat the oven to 180°C (350°F) Gas 4.

For the doughnuts, put the flour, xanthan gum, xylitol, baking powder, bicarbonate of soda/baking soda, cinnamon and salt in a large bowl. Stir with a balloon whisk.

Put the milk and vinegar in a small bowl; you will see a kind of 'buttermilk' start to form after a couple of minutes. Once this happens, add the sunflower oil, apple purée/applesauce and vanilla extract. Pour the wet mixture into the bowl of dry ingredients and you should see some bubbles form – this is what will make the doughnuts nice and fluffy! Use the whisk again to stir really gently, and stop as soon as the mixtures have combined.

If you have a piping/pastry bag, fill the bag with the mixture. If not, fold down your sandwich bag a few times and using a spoon, scoop the mixture into one bottom corner of the bag. Twist the end of the bag to prevent any air from coming in, then use a pair of scissors to snip off the filled corner of the bag – you'll want the cut to be about 1 cm/½ inch long. Pipe the mixture into the holes of the doughnut pan(s). Bake in the preheated oven for 5–6 minutes and keep an eye on them – they are so small that they bake very quickly.

For the cinnamon 'sugar', melt the sunflower spread and put in a bowl. Separately, combine the cinnamon and sweetener. Remove the baked doughnuts from the pan(s) and dip the top of each one into the melted sunflower spread, then straight into the cinnamon 'sugar'. Serve immediately – they taste best when straight from the oven, but they will also keep for about 2 days in an airtight container.

Sometimes, you want a sweet, chocolatey fix to end your day with but have neither the time nor the energy to go into full baking mode. This recipe makes enough cake for one person, so you're not left with a ton of waste or second helpings to tempt you away from your healthy intentions. There's also minimal clean-up involved, so it's ideal for whipping up just before your favourite TV show's about to start.

single-serving chocolate cake

SERVES 1

1 tablespoon ground flaxseeds/linseeds

3 tablespoons gluten-free plain/all-purpose flour

1 tablespoon unsweetened cocoa powder

1 tablespoon xylitol or stevia

¼ teaspoon baking powder

a pinch of salt (optional)

2 tablespoons almond milk

1 teaspoon nut butter of choice

1½ tablespoons dark/bittersweet chocolate chips

1 ceramic mug or large ramekin – microwave- or oven-safe, depending on your chosen baking method

Put the flaxseeds/linseeds and 3 tablespoons water in a small bowl. Whisk the seeds into the water with a fork until the mixture starts to feel like the consistency of a beaten egg – in fact, what you have is a 'flax egg' that plays the same role as an egg in plant-based baking recipes. Place in the refrigerator.

You can use a microwave or an oven for this recipe. If using an oven, preheat it to 180°C (350°F) Gas 4.

In your chosen mug or ramekin, combine the flour, cocoa powder, sweetener, baking powder and salt, if using. Add the 'flax egg', almond milk and nut butter and stir until smooth. Add the chocolate chips – you can either let these sit on top so that they seep into the cake when melted, or you can mix them in so they're evenly distributed throughout the cake.

If using a microwave oven, microwave the cake on high for about 45–60 seconds, until cooked through. If using an oven, bake for 5–6 minutes – no more than that, because it tastes best when the centre is still slightly gooey.

These crispie cakes are so simple, yet so addictive and impossible not to like. This is a good treat to give to someone if you're really trying to show them that living healthily while still enjoying indulgent foods from time to time is possible. In other words, it's a converter.

no-bake crispie cakes

MAKES 24

100 g/3½ oz. dark/bittersweet chocolate, chopped

60 ml/¼ cup coconut oil or 60 g/¼ cup non-hydrogenated sunflower spread

¼ teaspoon sea salt

110 g/2 cups plain corn flakes, with no added sugar

2 x 12-hole muffin pans, lined with paper cases/liners

Put the chocolate, coconut oil and salt in a heatproof bowl over a saucepan of barely simmering water. Leave until melted and completely smooth.

Tip the corn flakes into the melted chocolate. Mix thoroughly with a wooden spoon and don't be afraid to crush some of the corn flakes. Scoop a generous tablespoon of the mixture into each muffin case/liner, patting the mixture down as you go. Put the whole muffin pans in the freezer for 15 minutes.

Remove the cakes from the freezer just before serving. Store them in the freezer for up to 2 weeks.

desserts
and ices

These soft, gooey fondants have a dark secret; they are made with black beans, which means they are not only utterly delicious but also good for you. Black beans are packed with protein and fibre and help to regulate blood-sugar levels, so indulge yourself with this guilt-free dessert.

secretive chocolate fondants

MAKES 10–12

400-g/14-oz. can black beans

40 g/4 tablespoons gluten-free flour (buckwheat or quinoa work well)

4 tablespoons unsweetened cocoa powder

½ teaspoon baking powder

¼ teaspoon sea salt

90 ml/⅓ cup pure maple syrup or agave syrup

2 tablespoons xylitol or other granulated sweetener (stevia is not advisable in this recipe)

45 ml/¼ cup coconut oil

2 teaspoons pure vanilla extract

2 teaspoons grated orange zest or orange oil (or coffee extract, peppermint oil or other flavouring of choice)

130 g/¾ cup dark/bittersweet chocolate chips, or finely chopped dark/bittersweet chocolate

food processor or blender

10–12 ramekins

Preheat the oven to 180°C (350°F) Gas 4.

Drain the beans well, then put in a food processor or blender and blitz until completely smooth. Add the remaining ingredients, including most of the chocolate chips, and blitz again until everything is well incorporated and the chips aren't visible any more.

Divide the mixture between the ramekins, filling them only two-thirds full. You don't need to grease the ramekins before filling them. Scatter the last of the chocolate chips on top.

Bake in the preheated oven for about 15 minutes. Allow to cool for 5 minutes before digging right in – they should be really gooey and soft on the inside. They are best served immediately, but will keep for 5–6 hours at room temperature. You can also keep them refrigerated for 2–3 days and heat them for 5 minutes as needed.

SERVES 10

For the pastry

225 g/1¾ cups white spelt
    flour (for a wheat- and
    gluten-free alternative,
    see page 123)

a pinch of sea salt

3 teaspoons xylitol

50 g/3 tablespoons dairy-free
    butter, e.g. sunflower
    spread

60 g/¼ cup hard white
    vegetable shortening (it is
    crucial that you get the
    hardest one you can find)

1 egg, beaten together with
    1 teaspoon water

For the frangipane filling

70 g/½ cup pecans

80 g/⅔ cup blanched
    almonds

70 g/½ cup cashews

250 g/8¾ oz. dairy-free
    butter, e.g. sunflower
    or soy spread

40 g/3 tablespoons coconut
    oil

200 g/1 cup xylitol

grated zest of a lemon

3 eggs, lightly beaten

small handful of rice flour

pinch of sea salt

5 nectarines

sugar-free apricot jam,
    to glaze

food processor or blender

*20-cm/8-in. tart pan baking
    beans*

Stone fruit works brilliantly here, as once baked, their flavour
and texture mellows out and their juices run down into the
frangipane base, making for a deliciously moist and chewy tart.
You can swap the nectarines for plums, peaches, cherries or
pretty much any other stone fruit.

nectarine frangipane tart

To make the pastry, follow the method for the Lemon Tart on page 123 until
you have blind-baked the tart and taken it out to cool. Leave the oven on.

To make the frangipane filling, spread the pecans, almonds and cashews
out on a baking sheet and bake in the oven for about 8 minutes, or until
they have gone a shade darker. Allow to cool, then blitz in a food processor.
You want to keep them a little chunky, so don't grind them to a powder –
about 10–15 seconds will probably do it. Set aside.

Put the butter, coconut oil, xylitol and lemon zest in the food processor.
Blitz until light and fluffy. Remove to a large mixing bowl and beat in the
eggs, rice flour, salt and, finally, the cooled nuts. Allow to cool and set in
the fridge for at least 10 minutes.

When ready to bake, cut segments out of the nectarines. Spread the
frangipane mixture over the blind-baked tart shell and arrange the
nectarine segments on top in a fan pattern. Bake in the oven for about
45–55 minutes. The edges usually brown faster than the middle so cover
them with foil after about 25 minutes, or when golden.

Remove the tart from the oven when the middle has browned and
firmed up but is still a little wobbly when you gently shake it. Once cool,
mix some of the apricot jam with a little hot water and, using a pastry
brush, glaze the nectarines. Serve immediately.

Making a tart free of sugar, wheat and dairy that tastes as good as the normal one might seem impossible but this recipe really works.

lemon tart

SERVES 10–12

For the pastry

225 g/1¾ cups white spelt flour or gluten-free flour blend, or to make your own, combine 100 g/¾ cup rice flour, 70 g/¾ cup cornflour/cornstarch, 55 g/½ cup potato flour and 1 teaspoon xanthan gum

a pinch of sea salt

1 dessertspoon xylitol

50 g/3 tablespoons dairy-free butter, e.g. sunflower spread

60 g/¼ cup hard white vegetable shortening (it is crucial that you get the hardest one you can find)

1 egg, beaten together with 1 teaspoon water

For the filling

finely grated zest and juice of 3 lemons

juice of 1 orange

120 g/⅔ cup xylitol

4 eggs

160 ml/⅔ cup soy cream/creamer

soy yogurt and raspberries, to serve

20-cm/8-in. tart pan

baking beans

The pastry ingredients must be as cold as possible, especially the butter and shortening, so refrigerate until needed.

Sift the flour (and xanthan gum if you are making the gluten-free version) and salt into a large bowl. Add the xylitol, butter and shortening and cut into small chunks with a knife. Rub the butter and shortening into the flour until it resembles breadcrumbs. You can also do this in a food processor. Add a tablespoon of the egg mixture and fork the mixture together. If it is still crumbly and not coming together, add a little more liquid, being careful not to overdo it. Bring the dough together with your hands to a smooth ball. For the gluten-free version, you will need to squeeze and knead the pastry a little. If it is still crumbly, it needs a little more egg mixture. Gently flatten into a round, wrap in clingfilm/plastic wrap and refrigerate until cold.

Preheat the oven to 180°C (350°F) Gas 4.

Gluten-free pastry can be difficult to handle, so roll it out between 2 sheets of floured clingfilm/plastic wrap. Whichever pastry you have made, roll it out until 1 cm/⅜ in. thick, working quickly and handling it as little as possible. To line the tart pan, remove the top layer of film/wrap and roll the pastry over your rolling pin with the bottom sheet of film/wrap still on it. Lay the sheet of pastry over the pan with the film/wrap uppermost. Remove the film/wrap.

The gluten-free pastry will tear and crumble as you transfer it to the pan but this is quite normal, and although it looks like a shambles now it will be fine once blind-baked. Patch it up with the pieces that have fallen off and push the pastry into the pan, making sure it is an even thickness and there are no cracks. Prick the base with a fork. Line the pastry shell with parchment paper and fill with baking beans.

Blind bake in the preheated oven for about 20 minutes. (Leave the oven on.) Remove the paper and beans and brush the base and sides of the shell with egg mixture. Return to the oven and bake for a further 5–10 minutes until the base is beginning to brown. Remove and cool on a wire rack.

To make the filling, whisk the citrus zest, juices and xylitol in a pan and gently heat until the xylitol has just dissolved. Let cool, then whisk in the eggs and soy cream/creamer. Place the tart shell in the oven, then pour the filling in, right up to the top. Bake until the filling is just firm – about 20 minutes.

Convincing people that food, especially desserts, made without sugar can actually taste good, let alone delicious, is an almost impossible task. After tasting this chocolate tart, however, even the greatest cynics will beg you for the recipe, as well as another slice!

chocolate tart

SERVES 10–12

sea salt

100 g/3½ oz. dark/ bittersweet chocolate, at least 70% cocoa solids

For the base

10 pitted dates

150 g/1 cup pecans, lightly roasted

125 g/4 oz. Scottish oat cakes

1 teaspoon pure vanilla extract

2 tablespoons agave syrup

2 tablespoons coconut oil

3 teaspoons unsweetened cocoa powder

a pinch of sea salt

For the filling

3 avocados, not too firm

½ teaspoon sea salt

6 tablespoons agave syrup

1 tablespoon carob powder

5 tablespoons unsweetened cocoa powder

2 teaspoons pure vanilla extract

3 tablespoons date syrup

4 tablespoons coconut oil

20-cm/8-in. springform pan, base-lined with parchment paper

food processor or blender

To make the base, blitz the dates in a food processor, then add the rest of the ingredients and a pinch of salt and blitz until everything comes together into a sticky ball.

Press into the baking pan so that you have an even and smooth base for the tart. Refrigerate for 30 minutes or freeze for 15 minutes until set.

To make the filling, cut the avocados in half, remove the stones/pits and scoop the flesh into a food processor. Add the salt, the remaining ingredients apart from the coconut oil, and blitz until smooth.

Melt the coconut oil in a pan over the lowest heat possible – this will only take a few moments. Turn on the food processor and pour the coconut oil into the mixture through the funnel. Once combined, pour the mixture onto the set tart base and smooth out the top. Refrigerate for at least 2 hours, or if you want it to set quickly, freeze it.

When you are ready to serve, warm the chocolate to just above room temperature to make it easier to grate. I find leaving it beside the oven when you are cooking for about 10 minutes does the trick. You want the chocolate to be just beginning to soften – not in any way gooey or melting, just not rock solid, so it grates easily in long strips.

Pop the tart out of the baking pan and transfer to a plate. Liberally grate the chocolate over, so it piles up high. The tart should be served fridge-cold so that it stays reasonably firm. It keeps wonderfully well and can easily be made a day in advance.

The great thing about raw desserts is that you can be a lot looser when preparing them, feeling free to alter as you want; because nothing is baked, there's no need to be as precise with your measurements. Consider this recipe as a guideline – if you want to add some more sweetener, or switch up the mint for orange extract for example, feel free. Though this recipe may look complicated, don't be intimidated – essentially, it's blending 3 rounds of ingredients in the food processor, and using your freezer or fridge to set them.

raw tartlets

MAKES 4

145 g/1 cup almonds

135 g/¾ cup pitted dates

2 tablespoons unsweetened desiccated/dried shredded coconut, or more almonds

a pinch of sea salt

2 teaspoons coconut oil

For the mint chocolate filling
(to fill 2 tarts)

1 large banana

60 ml/¼ cup coconut oil

60 ml/¼ cup pure maple syrup

40 g/⅓ cup unsweetened cocoa powder

6 fresh mint leaves or ½ teaspoon mint extract

For the key lime filling
(to fill 2 tarts)

½ banana

1 small avocado

60 ml/¼ cup coconut oil

2½ tablespoons pure maple syrup

freshly squeezed juice of 1 lime

food processor or blender

4 tartlet moulds

Put the almonds in a food processor fitted with an 'S' blade and blitz until crumbly. Add the dates, desiccated coconut, salt and coconut oil and pulse until a smooth mixture forms. Remove the dough from the processor and divide it into 4. Press each portion into a tartlet mould so that it neatly lines the base and sides of the mould. Ideally you want the tartlet cases to be about 1 cm/½ inch thick all the way around, with plenty of room for the filling. Don't worry if you have a little extra dough – you can roll this into bite-size energy balls and save for a healthy snack later on.

For both the fillings, make sure the coconut oil is liquid. If it isn't, put it in a saucepan over low heat and allow to melt. Allow to cool completely, otherwise the hot oil will start to cook the other ingredients in the filling.

Place each set of filling ingredients in the food processor, one set at a time, and blitz until smooth. Divide each filling between 2 tartlet cases and freeze for at least 15 minutes to set.

Raw tarts will keep, in the freezer, for up to 2 weeks, so they're a great make-ahead option for tea and dinner parties.

The Italian name panna cotta actually means 'cooked cream', and it's exactly that – cooked milk with cream thickened with gelatine. This recipe uses plant milk and cream as well as the amazing seaweed gelatine agar-agar. This is a very light, creamy and wobbly dessert – it takes only a couple of minutes to make it and some patience until it cools in the fridge!

panna cotta

SERVES 3

220 ml/1 cup vanilla oat milk

220 ml/1 cup oat cream

1 heaped teaspoon agar-agar flakes

¼ teaspoon bourbon vanilla powder

70 g/¼ cup agave syrup

For the sauce

3 tablespoons hazelnut butter

1 teaspoon unsweetened cocoa powder

2 tablespoons agave syrup

a little nut milk or water, if necessary

dariole moulds or small ramekins

In a saucepan, mix the oat milk and oat cream and add the agar-agar. Bring to the boil, then lower the heat and cook for 5 minutes, or until the agar melts and you can't see any flakes left. Whisk in the vanilla powder and agave syrup and let the mixture boil again. Pour into dariole moulds or small ramekins and refrigerate for at least 1 hour before serving.

Turn each out of the mould onto a plate and, if necessary, run a knife around the edges to loosen them.

To make the sauce, mix together the first 3 ingredients until smooth and not too thick, so that when you pour the sauce over the panna cotta, it should slowly start to slide down its sides. Add a little nut milk or water to thin it down, if necessary.

Oat milk and cream can be substituted with soya/soy milk and cream with the same results. The sauce gives it extra nut flavour and sweetness, so don't omit it!

EACH RECIPE SERVES 1

For autumn-spiced chia pudding

1 tablespoon chia seeds

100 ml/6 tablespoons almond milk

freshly squeezed juice of 1 carrot

¼ teaspoon ground ginger

¼ teaspoon ground cloves

¼ teaspoon grated nutmeg

½ teaspoon ground cinnamon

1 tablespoon pure maple syrup, agave syrup or coconut nectar

For vanilla and coconut chia pudding

1 tablespoon chia seeds

125 ml/½ cup almond milk

3 tablespoons unsweetened desiccated/dried shredded coconut

1 teaspoon pure vanilla extract

For chocolate chia pudding

1 tablespoon chia seeds

125 ml/½ cup almond milk

1½ tablespoons unsweetened cocoa powder

2 tablespoons pure maple syrup

Chia pudding is a great alternative to oatmeal in the morning – it's very filling and also less starchy. Chia seeds themselves are tasteless, so the pudding will take on whatever flavour you give the liquid. Get creative!

chia pudding

Put the chia seeds and milk in an airtight container and stir well to combine, making sure there are no clumps. Set aside for 10 minutes – the seeds will start to expand.

Add the remaining ingredients, stir again, and refrigerate: for 1 hour if you like it thin, or overnight if you like it thick and comforting, almost like oatmeal. Keep it in the fridge (for up to 5 days) and steal a few spoonfuls when you need a little sweet pick-me-up.

This recipe is not only sugar-free but also dairy-free. To achieve that cloying, deeply creamy goodness of a cheesecake without dairy, the 'Tofutti' brand of dairy-free cream cheese is the answer. Made from soy and non-hydrogenated vegetable oils, it is identical to normal cream cheese in taste and texture.

cheesecake and sweet cherries

SERVES 10–12

500 g/1 lb. fresh cherries, stoned/pitted

4 tablespoons agave syrup

For the base

150 g/1 cup pecans

80 g/5½ tablespoons coconut oil

150 g/5 oz. Scottish oatcakes

2 tablespoons agave syrup

a good pinch of sea salt

For the filling

900 g/1 lb. 14 oz. Tofutti cream cheese

grated zest of 5 lemons and juice of 1

130 g/¾ cup xylitol

5 eggs

1 tablespoon rice flour

2 teaspoons pure vanilla extract

a pinch of sea salt

food processor or blender

20-cm/8-in. springform pan, lined with parchment paper

Preheat the oven to 180°C (350°F) Gas 4.

To make the base, roast the pecans on a baking sheet in the preheated oven for 10 minutes, or until they have gone a shade darker. Allow to cool slightly and leave the oven on.

Melt the coconut oil in a pan over the lowest heat possible – this will only take a few moments. Crush the oatcakes and roasted pecans in a food processor or in a sealed bag with a rolling pin, then transfer to a bowl with the melted coconut oil, agave syrup and salt and mix very well. Press into the baking pan so that you have an even and smooth base for the cheesecake.

To make the filling, put all the ingredients in a food processor and blitz until well combined. Pour the mixture onto the set cheesecake base and smooth out the top. Bake for about 45 minutes, or until it is just set and the middle is still a little wobbly. It will set further as it cools. Once completely cold, pop the cheesecake out of the baking pan and peel off the paper.

To serve, squash the cherries a little between your hands to release some of the juices. Add the agave syrup and mix together. Just before serving, pour onto the middle of the cheesecake and serve big wedges with the cherry liquid seeping down the sides.

EACH RECIPE SERVES 2

In advance

3 ripe bananas

a plastic bag

For berry ice-cream, add to the sliced bananas

160 g/1¼ cups frozen or fresh raspberries, sour-cherries or other berries

¼ teaspoon bourbon vanilla powder

2 tablespoons agave syrup

For double cocoa ice-cream, add to the sliced bananas

2 tablespoons unsweetened cocoa powder

2 tablespoons agave syrup

¼ teaspoon ground cinnamon

1 tablespoon raw cocoa nibs (mix in after blending)

For cappuccino-hazelnut ice-cream, add to the sliced bananas

2 tablespoons coffee powder

1 teaspoon coffee extract

2 tablespoons pure maple syrup

¼ teaspoon bourbon vanilla powder

4 tablespoons dry-roasted hazelnuts, chopped (mix in after blending)

high-speed blender

This type of ice-cream is very popular with raw foodies, but also becomes an instant favourite with anybody who tries it. It has the texture of old-fashioned ice cream and makes a great accompaniment to tarts and desserts, and can be made in a variety of delicious flavours that will be popular with grown-up guests. For a more child-friendly soft-serve recipe, see page 136.

classic ice cream

Peel the bananas and put them together in a plastic bag. Put the bag in the freezer and freeze them until they're completely hard. Take out of the freezer 10 minutes before using.

Slice the frozen bananas with a sharp knife. Place the banana slices and all other ingredients for your chosen ice-cream in a high-speed blender. Blend on the high setting and use the tamper (a tool that comes with the blender, which is used to push the ingredients down into the blades) to accelerate the blending process.

You might be able to make these ice-creams in a food processor, too, but it will probably take longer and turn out on the softer side because of the longer blending time. Serve immediately for a soft texture, or place in a freezer-proof container and freeze until firm.

EACH RECIPE SERVES 1

In advance

2 ripe bananas

a plastic bag

For vanilla soft-serve, add to the sliced bananas

a dash of pure vanilla extract

For chocolate soft-serve, add to the sliced bananas

1 generous tablespoon unsweetened cocoa powder

For strawberry soft serve, add to the sliced bananas

4 strawberries, fresh or frozen, chopped

This soft ice cream is a hit with children – and they'll never guess it's so good for them! Here you will find the classic Neapolitan flavours vanilla, chocolate and strawberry. Serve them straight from the food processor in sundae glasses for a super-quick dessert that everyone will love.

soft-serve sundaes

For the basic recipe, you will need 2 large bananas. Peel them, cut them in half and place in a sandwich bag to freeze for at least 3 hours. It's crucial that the bananas are frozen all the way through, otherwise you won't get an authentic ice-creamy texture.

Put the frozen bananas plus any chosen flavourings (see left) in a food processor and blitz until smooth. Make sure you hold on to your food processor when it's running at first, as it will shake! The soft serve will be done when it's completely smooth but still thick. The trick is in the timing: stop the food processor as soon as there are no more banana 'bits' in there, but don't leave it on too long, otherwise you'll have more of a melty smoothie than a soft-serve.

Transfer to sundae glasses and serve at once.

I scream, you scream, we all scream for ice cream! One of life's greatest pleasures has to be the cool, sweet, creamy smoothness of homemade ice cream. The notion that something this creamy and indulgent could actually be free of sugar and dairy and still taste this good, is just beyond most people.

cashew butter ice cream

SERVES 6

180 g/scant 1 cup xylitol

6 egg yolks

400 ml/1⅔ cups rice milk

400 ml/1⅔ cups soy cream/creamer

1 vanilla bean, split lengthways

200 g/1 scant cup cashew butter (available in supermarkets and health food stores)

3 tablespoons agave syrup

ice cream machine (optional)

For any ice cream, you start with a crème anglaise. Once you have this base, you can experiment with whatever ingredients you love: stewed fruit or melted chocolate (for stracciatella) are my favourites, but nuts or herbs are also good – in fact the possibilities are endless!

Put the xylitol and egg yolks in a bowl (or stand mixer) and, using an electric whisk, whisk until light and fluffy and pale yellow in colour.

Put the milk, soy cream/creamer and vanilla bean in a heavy-based saucepan and bring to the boil. After a minute, turn off the heat and allow to cool slightly.

Add the warm cream mixture to the egg mixture, whisking constantly and vigorously to prevent the egg from curdling. When it is all combined, pour the mixture back into the saucepan and place over low heat. Using a plastic spatula, stir the mixture constantly in a figure-eight motion. After about 5–10 minutes the mixture will have thickened and will coat the back of a wooden spoon – drag your finger across the back of the spoon and if the line holds and does not drip, you have got the right consistency. Be careful though, as it can turn into scrambled eggs very easily if the heat is too high.

If you have an ice cream machine, use this to churn the mixture according to the manufacturer's instructions.

If you don't have an ice cream machine, pour the mixture into a freezerproof container (wide, flat, metal trays work well, as the mixture freezes more quickly) and freeze.

After 30 minutes, or when the edges are beginning to freeze, remove the container from the freezer and whisk thoroughly to break down the ice crystals. Repeat this process twice more at 30-minute intervals. At this point, mix together the cashew butter and agave syrup and stir through the ice cream, so you have lovely cashew streaks and swirls, then return to the freezer to set fully.

Remove from the freezer about 15 minutes before serving so that it softens up a little – you want it smooth and creamy.

Frozen yogurt is going through a renaissance at the moment and it's not hard to see why. Fresh and light, with only a fraction of the fat of ice cream, it is the natural choice for the health conscious.

coconut frozen yogurt

SERVES 6–8

700 ml/1 lb. 8 oz. plain soy yogurt

340 ml/1½ cups coconut milk

100 ml/⅓ cup plus 1 tablespoon agave syrup

2 teaspoons lemon juice

desiccated coconut, to serve

strawberries, to serve

ice cream machine (optional)

Put the yogurt, milk, agave syrup and lemon juice in a bowl and mix until smooth. If you have an ice cream machine, use this to churn the mixture according to the manufacturer's instructions.

If you don't have an ice cream machine, pour the mixture into a freezerproof container (wide, flat, metal trays work well, as the mixture freezes more quickly) and freeze. After 30 minutes, or when the edges are beginning to freeze, remove the container from the freezer and whisk thoroughly to break down the ice crystals. Return to the freezer and repeat this process intermittently until completely frozen, but do not let it go rock hard, as you want to be able to scoop it out easily. If you want it super smooth, you can blitz it in a food processor when it is just frozen.

Scoop into a bowl and serve with strawberries and coconut over the top.

With this recipe you also have the added value of being able to use any leftover sorbet to make a killer mojito smoothie!

mojito sorbet

SERVES 6–8

170 g/scant 1 cup xylitol

5 sprigs of fresh mint, plus 2 tablespoons freshly chopped leaves

grated zest and freshly squeezed juice of 2 limes

ice cream machine (optional)

Put 500 ml/2 cups water, the xylitol and mint sprigs in a saucepan and bring to the boil. Reduce the heat to a minimum and simmer for 5 minutes.

Remove from the heat and strain the liquid, squeezing as much liquid as possible out of the sprigs. Add the lime zest immediately. Allow the mixture to cool slightly, then add the lime juice and mint leaves. Refrigerate to cool.

If you have an ice cream machine, use this to churn the mixture according to the manufacturer's instructions.

If you don't have an ice cream machine, pour the mixture into a freezer-proof container (wide, flat, metal trays work well, as the mixture freezes more quickly) and freeze. After 20 minutes, or when the edges are beginning to freeze, remove the container from the freezer and whisk thoroughly to break down the ice crystals. This will ensure a smooth sorbet. Return to the freezer and repeat this process intermittently until the sorbet is frozen.

index

credits

Picture credits

Tara Fisher
Page 33

William Reavell
Pages 4–5, 15, 42, 46–47, 63, 71, 117, 129, 134–135

Kate Whitaker
Pages 1, 27, 32, 38, 79–83, 98, 105, 116, 121–125, 133, 138, 141

Clare Winfield
Pages 2–3, 10, 12, 16–24, 28–31, 37, 41, 45, 49–59, 64–68, 72–76, 84–93, 101, 102, 106–114, 118, 126, 130, 137

Polly Wreford
Page 6, 34, 60, 94, 97

Recipe credits

Dunja Gulin
Cracker snacks with black sesame seeds, page 13
Buckwheat crackers, page 14
Pastry snails with spicy pumpkin filling, page 40
Courgette and walnut canapés, page 43
Cherry tomatoes filled with spinach pesto, page 47
Gooey chocolate cookies, page 62
Pure energy bars, page 70
Sugar-free Italian Easter buns, page 108
Panna cotta, page 128
Classic ice cream, page 135

Jenna Zoe
Rosemary breadsticks, page 17
Baked tortilla chips with necarine-tomato salsa, page 18
Cinema snacks, revisited, page 21
NYC-style glazed nuts, page 22
Bombay mix, page 25
Jalapeño onion rings, page 29
Healthified ketchup, page 29
Courgette UN-fries, page 30
Creole cauliflower, page 31
Edamame and miso dip, page 36
Courgette hummus, page 36
Party tartlets with hummus, page 44
Quinoa maki, page 48
Mango-avocado summer rolls with lime dipping sauce, page 51
Chard and cabbage wraps with peanut sauce, page 52
Aubergine and courgette roll-ups, page 55
Baby Gem lettuce wraps with sweet chilli sauce, page 56
Chocolate-chip coconut cookies, page 65
Oatmeal raisin cookies, page 66
Fig rolls, page 69
On-the-go snack bars, page 73
Walnut-goji Nanaimo bars, page 74
Coconut and spirulina energy bites, page 77
Chocolate-covered caramels, page 85
Almond butter cups, page 86
Cocoa-almond freezer fudge pops, page 89
Frozen cookie dough balls, page 90
Banana cake, page 100
Apple and cinnamon cake, page 103
Cinnamon buns, page 107
Mini baked doughnuts with cinnamon "sugar", page 111
Single serving chocolate cake, page 112
No-bake crispie cakes, page 115
Secretive chocolate fondants, page 119
Raw tartlets, page 127
Chia pudding, page 131
Soft-serve sundaes, page 136

Jordan and Jessica Bourke
Socca, page 26
Sweet potato hummus, page 39
Baba ghanoush, page 39
Borlotti bean purée, page 39
Flapjacks, page 78
Orange-zest brownies, page 81
Chocolate truffles, page 82
Moroccan orange cake, page 99
Apple, raisin and cinnamon muffins, page 104
Nectarine frangipane tart, page 120
Lemon tart, page 123
Chocolate tart, page 124
Cheesecake and sweet cherries, page 132
Cashew butter ice cream, page 139
Coconut frozen yogurt, page 140
Mojito sorbet, page 140

Amy Ruth Finegold
Beetroot herb dip with seeded amaranth crackers, page 35
Peanut butter quinoa cookies, page 61
Vegan chocolate fudge cake, page 95
Spice cake with mesquite flour, page 96